KNOW YOUR
HOCKEY!

KNOW YOUR HOCKEY!

THE AMAZING MULTIPLE-CHOICE QUIZ BOOK

JOHN A. WHITE

ARCTURUS

ARCTURUS

This edition published in 2008 by Arcturus Publishing Limited
26/27 Bickels Yard, 151–153 Bermondsey Street,
London SE1 3HA

ISBN: 978-1-84837-056-2

Printed in China

Contents

Know Your Hockey! is a celebration of the rich and colourful history of the 'world's fastest sport'. It has been designed as a multiple-choice quiz book spanning all eras of hockey with questions for young and old alike. Some questions are hard and some are easy but I hope all are interesting and entertaining. So sit back with family and friends and find out just how well you know your hockey!

John A. White

1 Who holds the Montreal Canadiens' franchise record for the most goals in a career?

A) Guy Lafleur   B) Maurice Richard

C) Jean Beliveau   D) Yvan Cournoyer

2 In 1999, the NHL introduced the Maurice 'Rocket' Richard Trophy. The Richard Trophy is awarded to the player who leads the NHL in goal scoring during the regular season. Who was the inaugural winner of the Richard Trophy?

A) Teemu Selanne   B) Mario Lemieux

C) Pavel Bure   D) Jaromir Jagr

3 Who was the first rookie in NHL history to record at least 100 points in a single regular season?

A) Mike Bossy   B) Dale Hawerchuk

C) Joe Nieuwendyk   D) Peter Stastny

4 With which team did Wendel Clark play the final game of his NHL career?

A) Detroit Red Wings   B) New York Islanders

C) Toronto Maple Leafs   D) Quebec Nordiques

5 Who holds the Buffalo Sabres franchise record for the most points in a single NHL regular season?

A) Dave Andreychuk   B) Pat LaFontaine

C) Alexander Mogilny   D) Gilbert Perreault

6 Who has won the most Stanley Cup rings as a player in NHL history?

A) Yvan Cournoyer   B) Henri Richard

C) Jean Beliveau   D) Maurice Richard

7 Who is the only player in NHL history to score three short-handed goals in a single regular season game?

A) Dave Keon B) Wayne Gretzky

C) Marcel Dionne D) Theo Fleury

8 Who was the last member of the Toronto Maple Leafs to be named to the NHL's First All-Star team?

A) Doug Gilmour B) Darryl Sittler

C) Borje Salming D) Tim Horton

9 Who was the first player in NHL history to score at least 50 goals in a season in six consecutive years?

A) Wayne Gretzky B) Guy Lafleur

C) Phil Esposito D) Mike Bossy

10 Who was named the most valuable player of the 2004 World Cup of Hockey?

A) Vincent Lecavalier B) Brett Hull

C) Mario Lemieux D) Jarome Iginla

11 Who was the first goaltender to be selected first overall in the NHL's Entry Draft?

A) Martin Brodeur B) Roberto Luongo

C) Rick DiPietro D) Patrick Roy

12 Who holds the Detroit Red Wings franchise record for the most career penalty minutes?

A) Ted Lindsay B) Chris Chelios

C) Bob Probert D) Gordie Howe

1   Who is the only member of the Montreal Canadiens to win the Hart Memorial Trophy as the NHL's most valuable player at least three times?

A) Howie Morenz   B) Jean Beliveau

C) Guy Lafleur   D) Maurice Richard

2   With which team did Hockey Hall of Fame member Paul Coffey play the final game of his NHL career?

A) Detroit Red Wings   B) Edmonton Oilers

C) Boston Bruins   D) Pittsburgh Penguins

3   Who is the youngest player ever to be inducted into the Hockey Hall of Fame?

A) Mario Lemieux   B) Bobby Orr

C) Howie Morenz   D) Guy Lafleur

4   Who is the oldest player in NHL history to record at least 100 points in a single regular season?

A) Wayne Gretzky   B) Gordie Howe

C) Mark Messier   D) Jean Beliveau

5   Name the NHL franchise that set a new record by finishing atop the NHL regular season standings for seven successive years.

A) Montreal Canadiens   B) Detroit Red Wings

C) Edmonton Oilers   D) Toronto Maple Leafs

6   Who played in an incredible 884 consecutive games as a member of the Chicago Blackhawks?

A) Stan Mikita   B) Denis Savard

C) Doug Wilson   D) Steve Larmer

7 Who was the last member of the New York Rangers to win the Calder Memorial Trophy as the NHL's rookie of the year?

A) Brian Leetch   B) Steve Vickers

C) Pat LaFointaine   D) Camille Henry

8 Who was the coach of the Montreal Canadiens the last time that the Habitants captured the Stanley Cup?

A) Jacques Lemaire   B) Jacques Demers

C) Pat Burns   D) Jean Perron

9 What was the name of Toronto's entry in the World Hockey Association?

A) Northmen   B) Toros

C) Blizzard   D) Shamrocks

10 Who is the only US-born player to be named to the NHL's First All-Star Team at least five times?

A) Mike Modano   B) Chris Chelios

C) Brian Leetch   D) Frank Brimsek

11 Name the Philadelphia Flyer star who was known as 'The Sultan of Slot'.

A) Eric Lindros   B) Tim Kerr

C) John LeClair   D) Gary Dornhoeffer

12 Who was the first player in NHL history to record at least 100 points in six consecutive seasons?

A) Phil Esposito   B) Wayne Gretzky

C) Bobby Orr   D) Guy Lafleur

1 Who is the longest serving captain in the history of the New Jersey Devils franchise?

A) Kirk Muller   B) Scott Niedermayer

C) Scott Stevens   D) Patrick Elias

2 Who is the youngest man to coach an NHL team?

A) Paul Maurice   B) Ted Nolan

C) Gary Green   D) Glen Sather

3 Who has scored the most career points in the Stanley Cup Playoffs as a member of the Montreal Canadiens?

A) Guy Lafleur   B) Henri Richard

C) Maurice Richard   D) Jean Beliveau

4 Who was the all time leading point producer in the short history of the World Hockey Association?

A) Bobby Hull   B) Anders Hedberg

C) Marc Tardif   D) Andre Lacroix

5 Who was the first goaltender to win the Hart Memorial Trophy as the NHL's most valuable player?

A) George Hainsworth   B) Turk Broda

C) Frank Brimsek   D) Roy Worters

6 Name the only player to score at least 500 NHL goals as a member of the Boston Bruins.

A) John Bucyk   B) Ray Bourque

C) Phil Esposito   D) Rick Middleton

7   Who holds the record for the fastest two goals by an individual in the NHL All-Star Game?

A) Mike Gartner   B) Vincent Damphousse

C) Owen Nolan   D) Dany Heatley

8   Who was the first US-born player to score five goals in an NHL regular season game?

A) Mark Pavelich   B) Joe Mullen

C) Neal Broten   D) Jeremy Roenick

9   Who is the only coach to win the Jack Adams Award as the NHL's coach of the year, in consecutive seasons?

A) Pat Burns   B) Fred Shero

C) Jacques Demers   D) Pat Quinn

10   Wayne Gretzky recorded the 1000th point of his NHL career in just his 424th NHL game. Who was the fastest to 1000 points prior to Gretzky shattering the record?

A) Marcel Dionne   B) Mike Bossy

C) Phil Esposito   D) Guy Lafleur

11   Who was the last member of the Toronto Maple Leafs to win the Lady Byng Trophy as the NHL's most gentlemanly player?

A) Dave Keon   B) Red Kelly

C) Ron Francis   D) Alexander Mogilny

12   Which NHL team originally selected Ken Dryden in the 1964 NHL Amateur Draft?

A) Toronto Maple Leafs   B) Boston Bruins

C) Montreal Canadiens   D) New York Rangers

1 Who was the first player in NHL history to record at least 100 points in a regular season for two different teams?

A) Jean Ratelle   B) Phil Esposito
C) Wayne Gretzky   D) Marcel Dionne

2 Who was the first player to record a hat-trick in the NHL All-Star Game?

A) Gordie Howe   B) Ted Lindsay
C) Jean Beliveau   D) Maurice Richard

3 Who was the first member of the Buffalo Sabres to record at least 100 points in a single NHL regular season?

A) Gilbert Perreault   B) Danny Gare
C) Rene Robert   D) Richard Martin

4 Name the two teams that have faced each other the most times in the NHL's Stanley Cup Finals.

A) Montreal and Boston   B) Toronto and Detroit
C) Toronto and Montreal   D) Montreal and Detroit

5 Name the only player in NHL history to score at least 30 power-play goals in a season twice in his career.

A) Wayne Gretzky   B) Brett Hull
C) Mike Bossy   D) Mario Lemieux

6 Who is the only member of the Calgary Flames to score five times in a single NHL regular season game?

A) Theo Fleury   B) Lanny McDonald
C) Joe Nieuwendyk   D) Gary Roberts

7 The NHL record for the most career points by a goaltender stands at 48. Who holds this record?

A) Ron Hextall   B) Tom Barrasso

C) Grant Fuhr   D) Ed Belfour

8 Who holds the NHL record for the most career goals in the Stanley Cup Finals?

A) Maurice Richard   B) Mark Messier

C) Jean Beliveau   D) Wayne Gretzky

9 What was the name of the defunct St. Louis franchise that took part in the 1934-35 NHL campaign?

A) Cardinals   B) Eagles

C) Sparrows   D) Hawks

10 For which NHL team did the legendary Bobby Hull play the final game of his NHL career?

A) Hartford Whalers   B) New York Rangers

C) Chicago Blackhawks   D) Winnipeg Jets

11 Who was the first player in NHL history to record at least 500 points during his career?

A) Howie Morenz   B) Syd Howe

C) Nels Stewart   D) Frank Boucher

12 Who was the first player in NHL history to win four major awards in a single season?

A) Wayne Gretzky   B) Bobby Orr

C) Stan Mikita   D) Gordie Howe

1 The NHL record for the most points in a single period of a game stands at six. Who holds this record?

A) Darryl Sittler   B) Mario Lemieux

C) Wayne Gretzky   D) Bryan Trottier

2 Who holds the Philadelphia Flyers record for the most points in a single NHL season?

A) Bobby Clarke   B) Eric Lindros

C) Bill Barber   D) Mark Recchi

3 Who is the only player in NHL history to receive ten penalties in a single game?

A) Gerry Hart   B) Jim Dorey

C) Chris Nilan   D) Tie Domi

4 Who is the longest serving coach in the franchise history of the Tampa Bay Lightning?

A) Jacques Demers   B) John Tortorella

C) Phil Esposito   D) Terry Crisp

5 Gordie Howe was named to the NHL's First All-Star Team 12 times during his illustrious career. Who is the only other forward to be named to the NHL's First Team at least ten times?

A) Bobby Hull   B) Wayne Gretzky

C) Mario Lemieux   D) Maurice Richard

6 The NHL record for goals allowed by a team in a single season stands at 446. Name the NHL franchise that holds this record?

A) Oakland Seals   B) Ottawa Senators

C) Kansas City Scouts   D) Washington Capitals

7 For which Ontario Hockey League team did defensive specialist Bob Gainey play his major junior hockey?

A) Kitchener Rangers   B) Kingston Canadians
C) Peterborough Petes   D) Cornwall Royals

8 Who is the only goaltender in NHL history to record three points in a single regular season game?

A) Curtis Joseph   B) Grant Fuhr
C) Jeff Reese   D) Ron Tugnett

9 Gilbert Perreault played 1,191 NHL games as a member of the Buffalo Sabres during his career. Who is the only other player to suit up for the Sabres in more than 1,000 games?

A) Dave Andreychuk   B) Danny Gare
C) Rob Ray   D) Craig Ramsay

10 Name the team that holds the NHL record for the most consecutive losses in the Stanley Cup Playoffs, with 16.

A) Los Angeles Kings   B) Chicago Blackhawks
C) Toronto Maple Leafs   D) San Jose Sharks

11 Who holds the NHL record for the most goals scored by a defenseman in a single season?

A) Paul Coffey   B) Al MacInnis
C) Bobby Orr   D) Raymond Bourque

12 Who holds the St. Louis Blues franchise record for the most points in a single NHL campaign?

A) Adam Oates   B) Brett Hull
C) Bernie Federko   D) Brendan Shanahan

1 Which NHL team is the only club in history to have three defensemen score at least 20 goals in the same season?

A) Washington Capitals   B) Edmonton Oilers

C) Detroit Red Wings   D) Pittsburgh Penguins

2 Who is the longest serving captain in the history of the St. Louis Blues NHL franchise?

A) Brett Hull   B) Brian Sutter

C) Barclay Plager   D) Red Berenson

3 Who is the only goaltender in NHL history to record two undefeated streaks of better than 25 games?

A) Pete Peeters   B) Bernie Parent

C) Gerry Cheevers   D) Dominik Hasek

4 The New York Islanders joined the NHL as an expansion team for the 1972-73 season. Which other expansion team joined the NHL that season?

A) Buffalo Sabres   B) Atlanta Flames

C) Kansas City Scouts   D) Cleveland Barons

5 Which NHL city hosted the NHL Entry Draft from 1963 until 1984 inclusive?

A) Toronto   B) New York

C) Detroit   D) Montreal

6 Who is the longest serving coach in the history of the Montreal Canadiens NHL franchise?

A) Toe Blake   B) Leo Dandurand

C) Dick Irvin   D) Scotty Bowman

7 The Detroit Red Wings of the 1950s featured perhaps the greatest forward line of the decade. Which one of the following was not a member of the Red Wings' famed 'Production Line'?

A) Gordie Howe   B) Alex Delvecchio
C) Ted Lindsay   D) Sid Abel

8 Wayne Gretzky scored 894 NHL regular season goals during his illustrious career. Name the player who ranks first in assists on Gretzky' goals.

A) Jari Kurri   B) Paul Coffey
C) Mark Messier   D) Glenn Anderson

9 With which World Hockey Association team did Gordie, Mark and Marty Howe make hockey history by becoming the first father and sons to play together professionally?

A) Hartford Whalers   B) Indianapolis Racers
C) Birmingham Bulls   D) Houston Aeros

10 Who played in a franchise-record 486 consecutive NHL games for the Toronto Maple Leafs?

A) Dave Keon   B) Darryl Sittler
C) Tim Horton   D) Borje Salming

11 Who was the first defenseman to win the Calder Memorial Trophy as the NHL's rookie of the year?

A) Bobby Orr   B) Kent Douglas
C) Jacques Laperriere   D) Red Kelly

12 Who was the first goaltender to win 16 games in a single Stanley Cup Playoff campaign?

A) Grant Fuhr   B) Patrick Roy
C) Billy Smith   D) Mike Vernon

1 Who holds the single season NHL record for the most goals by a defenseman in the Stanley Cup Playoffs?

A) Al MacInnis   B) Paul Coffey

C) Bobby Orr   D) Denis Potvin

2 Name the team that has produced the most scoring champions in the history of the NHL.

A) Montreal Canadiens   B) Pittsburgh Penguins

C) Boston Bruins   D) Chicago Blackhawks

3 Only three coaches in NHL history have been behind the bench for 500 or more victories with one team. Which one of the following did not win 500 games with one team?

A) Al Arbour   B) Billy Reay

C) Scotty Bowman   D) Toe Blake

4 Who were the first set of twins drafted in the NHL Entry Draft?

A) Henrik and Daniel Sedin

B) Rich and Ron Sutter

C) Patrik and Peter Sundstrom

D) Marian and Anton Stastny

5 Who is the only member of the Montreal Canadiens to score six goals in a single NHL game?

A) Maurice Richard   B) Bobby Rousseau

C) Howie Morenz   D) Newsy Lalonde

6 Who has recorded the most career shutouts in the franchise history of the Edmonton Oilers?

A) Andy Moog   B) Curtis Joseph

C) Tommy Salo   D) Grant Fuhr

7 For which Ontario Hockey League franchise did Joe Thornton play his major junior hockey?

A) Sudbury Wolves

B) Sarnia Sting

C) Belleville Bulls

D) Sault Ste. Marie Greyhounds

8 Who was the first European-trained player to win the Calder Memorial Trophy as the NHL's rookie of the year?

A) Sergei Makarov   B) Teemu Selanne

C) Pavel Bure   D) Peter Stastny

9 The youngest player to score five goals in a single NHL game was just 19 years old when he accomplished the feat. Name him.

A) Dale Hawerchuk   B) Jimmy Carson

C) Denis Savard   D) Don Murdoch

10 Name the NHL rookie who became the league's highest-paid player upon signing his first contract.

A) Bobby Orr   B) Wayne Gretzky

C) Jean Beliveau   D) Mario Lemieux

11 Which team holds the NHL record for the most victories in a single regular season?

A) Montreal Canadiens   B) Boston Bruins

C) Philadelphia Flyers   D) Detroit Red Wings

12 Who was the last NHL rookie to score three goals in his first NHL game?

A) Real Cloutier   B) Sidney Crosby

C) Marcel Dionne   D) Alexander Ovechkin

1   The Jack Adams Award was first introduced into the NHL in 1974, to honor the NHL's coach of the year. Who was the inaugural recipient of this prestigious award?

A) Fred Shero   B) Don Cherry

C) Scotty Bowman   D) Al Arbour

2   Wayne Gretzky was known as 'The Great One', but who was known as 'The Grate One'?

A) Ken Linseman   B) Esa Tikkanen

C) Theo Fleury   D) Keith Acton

3   Who holds the Philadelphia Flyers' franchise record for the most career penalty minutes?

A) Dave Shultz   B) Rick Tocchet

C) Bobby Clarke   D) Bob Kelly

4   Who is the only player in NHL history to score at least 40 goals and accumulate over 300 minutes in penalties in a single season?

A) Al Secord   B) Dave Williams

C) Kevin Stevens   D) Keith Tkachuk

5   Who was the first player in NHL history to score the Stanley Cup winning goal in back to back seasons?

A) Maurice Richard   B) George Armstrong

C) Mario Lemieux   D) Mike Bossy

6   Who is the only rookie in NHL history to score at least 30 power-play goals in a single regular season?

A) Teemu Selanne   B) Mario Lemieux

C) Mike Bossy   D) Joe Nieuwendyk

7 Who is the oldest netminder to record a shutout in an NHL regular season game?

A) Johnny Bower   B) Jacques Plante

C) Glenn Hall   D) Ed Belfour

8 During the depression years, the New York Rangers featured the forward line of Bill Cook, Bun Cook and Frank Boucher. What was this marvelous line's nickname?

A) The Bread Line   B) The Wonder Line

C) The Stamp Line   D) The Empire Line

9 For which Ontario Hockey League team did the Philadelphia Flyers' Mike Richards play his major junior hockey?

A) Sault Ste. Marie Greyhounds

B) Sarnia Sting

C) Kitchener Rangers

D) Plymouth Whalers

10 Who is the only US-born player in NHL history to score at least 50 goals in three consecutive seasons?

A) Joe Mullen   B) Jeremy Roenick

C) John LeClair   D) Mike Modano

11 The Toronto Maple Leafs franchise record for shutouts in a single regular season stands at 13. Who holds this impressive record?

A) Turk Broda   B) Johnny Bower

C) Mike Palmateer   D) Harry Lumley

12 Who was the coach of the Boston Bruins the last time they captured the Stanley Cup?

A) Don Cherry   B) Tom Johnson

C) Harry Sinden   D) Bep Guidolin

1   Boston Bruins' Bobby Orr established a new record for points in a single season by a defenseman when he recorded 64 points during the 1968-69 NHL season. Who held the record prior to Orr?

A) Doug Harvey   B) Pierre Pilote
C) Red Kelly   D) Bill Gadsby

2   Who was voted the most valuable player of the 1996 World Cup of Hockey?

A) Brett Hull   B) Wayne Gretzky
C) Steve Yzerman   D) Mike Richter

3   Who holds the Quebec Nordiques/Colorado Avalanche franchise record for the most points in a single regular season?

A) Joe Sakic   B) Peter Forsberg
C) Michel Goulet   D) Peter Stastny

4   Name the diminutive NHL forward who was dubbed 'The Little Giant'.

A) Marcel Dionne   B) Aurel Joliet
C) Camille Henry   D) Newsy Lalonde

5   Who is the longest-serving captain in the franchise history of the New York Rangers?

A) Mark Messier   B) Andy Bathgate
C) Bill Cook   D) Bob Nevin

6   Who was the first man to coach at least 1000 NHL games for one team?

A) Toronto's Punch Imlach
B) Montreal's Toe Blake
C) Chicago's Billy Reay
D) Montreal's Scotty Bowman

7 Only one first overall selection in the NHL's Entry Draft has gone on to win the Stanley Cup in his rookie year. Name him.

A) Denis Potvin   B) Guy Lafleur

C) Rejean Houle   D) Mel Bridgman

8 Wayne Gretzky has won the Hart Memorial Trophy a record nine times. Who is the only other player in NHL history to win the Hart as many as five times?

A) Mario Lemieux   B) Gordie Howe

C) Eddie Shore   D) Bobby Orr

9 How many times have the Boston Bruins captured the Stanley Cup?

A) 2   B) 3

C) 4   D) 5

10 For which Western Hockey League franchise did Anaheim's Ryan Getzlaf play his major junior hockey?

A) Kelowna Rockets   B) Saskatoon Blades

C) Red Deer Rebels   D) Calgary Hitmen

11 What was the name of the Vancouver franchise that was a member of the World Hockey Association from 1973 until 1975?

A) Blades   B) Blazers

C) Raiders   D) Bulldogs

12 Who holds the NHL record for the most career points in the Stanley Cup Finals?

A) Maurice Richard   B) Wayne Gretzky

C) Jean Beliveau   D) Gordie Howe

1 Maurice Richard was known famously as 'The Rocket'. What nickname was bestowed on 'The Rocket's' younger brother, Henri?

A) 'The Socket Rocket'   B) 'The Pocket Rocket'
C) 'The Missle'   D) 'The Little Rocket'

2 Who holds the Calgary Flames franchise record for the most games played with the team?

A) Jarome Iginla   B) Theo Fleury
C) Al MacInnis   D) Brad Marsh

3 Who was the last defenseman to win both the Hart Memorial Trophy as the NHL's most valuable player and the James Norris Trophy as the League's top defenseman in the same season?

A) Nicklas Lidstrom   B) Raymond Bourque
C) Chris Pronger   D) Bobby Orr

4 Who is the only member of the Detroit Red Wings to score six goals in a single NHL game?

A) Syd Howe   B) Sid Abel
C) John Ogrodnick   D) Danny Grant

5 Name the only Original Six NHL team that has not had a player win the James Norris Trophy as the NHL's outstanding defenseman.

A) New York Rangers   B) Toronto Maple Leafs
C) Chicago Blackhawks   D) Boston Bruins

6 Who is the only goaltender in NHL history to be named to the NHL's First All-Star Team with three different teams?

A) Jacques Plante   B) Glenn Hall
C) Terry Sawchuk   D) Dominik Hasek

7 Who was the first General Manager in the Florida Panthers franchise history?

A) Bryan Murray   B) Bobby Clarke

C) Doug MacLean   D) Rick Dudley

8 How many times has Great Britain captured the Olympic Gold Medal in hockey?

A) 0   B) 1

C) 2   D) 3

9 Who was the last member of the Chicago Blackhawks to be selected to the NHL's First All-Star team?

A) Ed Belfour   B) Doug Wilson

C) Chris Chelios   D) Denis Savard

10 Who succeeded the retired Maurice Richard as captain of the Montreal Canadiens for the 1960-61 NHL season?

A) Jean Beliveau   B) Butch Bouchard

C) Doug Harvey   D) Henri Richard

11 Who was the last member of the Detroit Red Wings to lead the NHL in goal scoring in a single regular season?

A) Norm Ullman   B) Ted Lindsay

C) Steve Yzerman   D) Gordie Howe

12 Who was the last player to lead the NHL in penalty minutes for three consecutive seasons?

A) Dave Schultz   B) Bob Probert

C) Tie Domi   D) Rob Ray

1 Who was the first player to score three penalty-shot goals in a single NHL season?

A) Pavel Bure   B) Mario Lemieux

C) Mats Sundin   D) Teemu Selanne

2 Who was often referred to as the 'Ultimate Bruin'?

A) Milt Schmidt   B) Eddie Shore

C) Bobby Orr   D) Johnny Bucyk

3 Wayne Gretzky was named to either the NHL's First or Second All-Star Team at center a record 15 times during his career. Who is the only other centerman to make either the First or Second All-Star Team as many as ten times?

A) Stan Mikita   B) Phil Esposito

C) Jean Beliveau   D) Mario Lemieux

4 Who is the only goaltender in NHL history to win the Vezina Trophy five consecutive times?

A) Ken Dryden   B) Martin Brodeur

C) Dominik Hasek   D) Jacques Plante

5 Who is the longest serving head coach in the history of the Buffalo Sabres franchise?

A) Lindy Ruff   B) Scotty Bowman

C) Punch Imlach   D) Floyd Smith

6 Who is the only Swedish-born player to win the Hart Memorial Trophy as the NHL's most valuable player?

A) Markus Naslund   B) Nicklas Lidstrom

C) Mats Sundin   D) Peter Forsberg

7 The New Jersey Devils captured their first Stanley Cup in 1995. Who was the coach behind the bench for the Devils' first Stanley Cup Championship?

A) Jacques Lemaire   B) Herb Brooks
C) Pat Burns   D) Larry Robinson

8 Bobby Orr was the first defenseman in NHL history to record at least 100 points in a single season. Who was next defenseman to accomplish the feat?

A) Raymond Bourque   B) Paul Coffey
C) Al MacInnis   D) Denis Potvin

9 Who is the only player in NHL history to lead the league in goal scoring for a record seven seasons?

A) Wayne Gretzky   B) Guy Lafleur
C) Bobby Hull   D) Phil Esposito

10 How many times did Gordie Howe capture the Art Ross Trophy as the NHL's leading point producer?

A) 4   B) 5
C) 6   D) 7

11 The Pittsburgh Penguins chose Jaromir Jagr with the fifth overall selection of the 1990 NHL Entry Draft. Who was chosen first overall in the 1990 Entry Draft?

A) Owen Nolan   B) Eric Lindros
C) Roman Hamrlik   D) Alexander Daigle

12 Who was the Toronto Maple Leafs' opponent in both the first game played at Maple Leaf Gardens and the last game played at the fabled arena?

A) Montreal Canadiens   B) Detroit Red Wings
C) Boston Bruins   D) Chicago Blackhawks

1   With which Ontario Hockey League franchise did
Patrick Kane play his major junior hockey?

A) Sarnia Sting   B) Plymouth Whalers
C) London Knights   D) Kitchener Rangers

2   Who was the first member of the St. Louis Blues to
score at least 50 goals in a single NHL season?

A) Brett Hull   B) Bernie Federko
C) Wayne Babych   D) Brian Sutter

3   The World Hockey Association commenced play in
1972. Name the team that captured the Avco Cup
as WHA Champion, in the league's first year of
operation.

A) Winnipeg Jets   B) New England Whalers
C) Houston Aeros   D) Quebec Nordiques

4   Who holds the NHL record for the most points in a
single season, for a left winger?

A) Luc Robitaille   B) Michel Goulet
C) Kevin Stevens   D) Dave Andreychuk

5   Wayne Gretzky scored at least 40 goals in a season
a record 12 times during his NHL career while Mario
Lemieux scored at least 40 goals in a season on ten
occasions. Who is the only other player in NHL history
to score at least 40 goals in a season ten times in his
NHL career?

A) Guy Lafleur   B) Marcel Dionne
C) Mike Bossy   D) Mike Gartner

6   Who has recorded the most career shutouts in the
franchise history of the Montreal Canadiens?

A) Ken Dryden   B) Patrick Roy
C) Jacques Plante   D) George Hainsworth

7   How many times has Canada captured the Olympic Gold Medal in hockey?

A) 4   B) 5
C) 6   D) 7

8   Who is the only goaltender in NHL history to record at least 15 shutouts in a season, twice in his career?

A) Alec Connell   B) Tony Esposito
C) George Hainsworth   D) Terry Sawchuk

9   What was the name of the Pittsburgh franchise that was a member of the NHL from 1925 until 1930?

A) Bulldogs   B) Pirates
C) Steelers   D) Panthers

10   With which team did Tie Domi begin his NHL career?

A) Toronto Maple Leafs   B) Winnipeg Jets
C) New York Rangers   D) Pittsburgh Penguins

11   Name the Hockey Hall of Fame defenseman who was nicknamed 'The Edmonton Express'.

A) Paul Coffey   B) Doug Harvey
C) Eddie Shore   D) Bill Gadsby

12   Who is the longest serving captain in the franchise history of the Washington Capitals?

A) Dale Hunter   B) Kevin Hatcher
C) Rod Langway   D) Mike Gartner

1. Who was the last member of the Toronto Maple Leafs to win the Calder Memorial Trophy as the NHL's rookie of the year?

   A) Kent Douglas   B) Wendel Clark
   C) Dave Keon   D) Brit Selby

2. Who is the only member of the New York Rangers to record at least seven points in a single NHL game?

   A) Rod Gilbert   B) Walt Tkaczuk
   C) Jean Ratelle   D) Steve Vickers

3. Who was the youngest netminder to appear in an NHL All-Star Game?

   A) Harry Lumley   B) Tom Barrasso
   C) Grant Fuhr   D) Patrick Roy

4. The NHL record for the fastest to score 100 goals from the beginning of a career stands at 129 games. Who holds this impressive record?

   A) Wayne Gretzky   B) Teemu Selanne
   C) Alexander Ovechkin   D) Mike Bossy

5. Who was the last player to lead the NHL in goal scoring for three years in succession?

   A) Mario Lemieux   B) Wayne Gretzky
   C) Pavel Bure   D) Brett Hull

6. Who was the last member of the Chicago Blackhawks to be named to the NHL's First All-Star Team?

   A) Ed Belfour   B) Denis Savard
   C) Chris Chelios   D) Doug Wilson

7 Who was the only player to play on at least four Stanley Cup Championship teams during the 1990s?

A) Mike Keane   B) Larry Murphy

C) Claude Lemieux   D) Joe Nieuwendyk

8 Who holds the NHL record for the most career power-play goals?

A) Brett Hull   B) Dave Andreychuk

C) Jari Kurri   D) Phil Esposito

9 Who is the only left winger in NHL history to record over 800 assists during his career?

A) Luc Robitaille   B) Johnny Bucyk

C) Bobby Hull   D) Brendan Shanahan

10 Which nation did the United States defeat in the final game of the 1980 Winter Olympics to secure the gold medal in hockey?

A) Canada   B) Finland

C) Soviet Union   D) Sweden

11 Who was the last player to record at least 150 points in a single NHL season?

A) Wayne Gretzky   B) Jaromir Jagr

C) Steve Yzerman   D) Mario Lemieux

12 Maurice 'Rocket' Richard scored the 500th goal of his NHL career on October 19th, 1957. Name the Hall of Fame goaltender that Richard beat for this historic goal.

A) Glenn Hall   B) Terry Sawchuk

C) Gump Worsley   D) Johnny Bower

1 Who was the first Swedish-born player to score at least 50 goals in a single NHL season?

A) Kent Nilsson   B) Mats Sundin
C) Willy Lidstrom   D) Hakan Loob

2 The Pittsburgh Penguins chose Mario Lemieux with the first pick of the 1984 NHL Entry Draft. Who was selected second overall in 1984?

A) Steve Yzerman   B) Kirk Muller
C) Gary Suter   D) Pat LaFontaine

3 Who holds the NHL record for the most game-winning goals in one Stanley Cup Playoff campaign?

A) Joe Sakic   B) Mike Bossy
C) Brad Richards   D) Jari Kurri

4 Who is the only player in NHL history to be inducted into the Hockey Hall of Fame immediately following his final game in the NHL?

A) Dit Clapper   B) Howie Morenz
C) Newsy Lalonde   D) Eddie Shore

5 For which Western Hockey League team did Scott Niedermayer play his major junior hockey?

A) Prince Albert Raiders   B) Kamloops Blazers
C) Portland Winter Hawks   D) Kelowna Rockets

6 Who was the last member of the Montreal Canadiens to record at least 100 points in a single NHL season?

A) Mats Naslund   B) Guy Lafleur
C) Stephane Richer   D) Pierre Larouche

7 Who was the coach of the Edmonton Oilers the last time they captured the Stanley Cup?

A) John Muckler   B) Ted Green

C) Glen Sather   D) Ron Low

8 On April 7th, 1987, Wayne Gretzky registered an NHL record tying six assists in a single Stanley Cup Playoff game. With whom does Gretzky share this record?

A) Doug Gilmour   B) Patrik Sundstrom

C) Mikko Leinonen   D) Risto Siltanen

9 Who is the only goaltender in history to play in the NHL in four different decades?

A) Johnny Bower   B) Gump Worsley

C) Terry Sawchuk   D) Glenn Hall

10 Who won the last Stanley Cup prior to the formation of the NHL in 1917?

A) Seattle Metropolitans

B) Montreal Canadiens

C) Ottawa Senators

D) Vancouver Millionaires

11 Goaltenders Martin Brodeur and Curtis Joseph represented Canada at the 2002 Winter Olympic Games in Salt Lake City, Utah. Who was the third goaltender named to Canada's 2002 Olympic squad?

A) Marty Turco   B) Jose Theodore

C) Jean-Sebastien Giguere   D) Ed Belfour

12 With which team did Jean-Sebastian Giguere begin his NHL career?

A) Anaheim Mighty Ducks   B) Calgary Flames

C) Edmonton Oilers   D) Hartford Whalers

1 Who is the only player to score over 400 NHL regular season goals as a member of the Philadelphia Flyers?

A) Bill Barber   B) Tim Kerr
C) Bobby Clarke   D) Eric Lindros

2 Who has played the most NHL regular season games as a member of the Los Angeles Kings?

A) Luc Robitaille   B) Marcel Dionne
C) Larry Murphy   D) Dave Taylor

3 What was the name of Ottawa's entry in the World Hockey Association?

A) Capitals   B) Nationals
C) Senators   D) Terriers

4 Name the Hockey Hall of Fame member who was once described in a newspaper article as 'Nureyev on ice'.

A) Bobby Orr   B) Guy Lafleur
C) Wayne Gretzky   D) Mario Lemieux

5 In which round did the Detroit Red Wings select Pavel Datsyuk in the 1998 NHL Entry Draft?

A) 5th   B) 6th
C) 7th   D) 8th

6 Name the team that was granted an NHL franchise to begin the 1999-2000 season, thus making the NHL a 28-team league.

A) Nashville Predators   B) Atlanta Thrashers
C) Columbus Blue Jackets   D) Minnesota Wild

7 Bobby Orr of the Boston Bruins recorded a plus 124 during the 1970-71 NHL season. Who is the only other player in NHL history to register at least a plus 120 in a single season?

A) Denis Potvin   B) Paul Coffey
C) Nicklas Lidstrom   D) Larry Robinson

8 Who was the last New York Ranger goaltender to be selected to the NHL's First All-Star Team?

A) Ed Giacomin   B) Mike Richter
C) Henrik Lundqvist   D) John Vanbiesbrouck

9 Which of the Original Six teams has the Detroit Red Wings faced the most times in the Stanley Cup Final?

A) Montreal Canadiens   B) Toronto Maple Leafs
C) Boston Bruins   D) Chicago Blackhawks

10 Who was the first coach in NHL history to lead his team to the Stanley Cup Championship at least five times?

A) Hap Day   B) Toe Blake
C) Dick Irvin   D) Jack Adams

11 During his illustrious career, there were three occasions when Terry Sawchuk recorded 12 shutouts in a season for the Detroit Red Wings. Who is the only other Red Wing to register 12 shutouts in a season?

A) Dominik Hasek   B) Roger Crozier
C) Harry Lumley   D) Glenn Hall

12 Who scored the most career regular season goals in the short history of the World Hockey Association?

A) Anders Hedberg   B) Bobby Hull
C) Marc Tardif   D) Andre Lacroix

1 Who is the only member of the New Jersey Devils to register six points in a single NHL regular season game?

A) Patrik Elias   B) John MacLean
C) Kirk Muller   D) Scott Gomez

2 Who holds the Toronto Maple Leafs franchise record for the most points in a single NHL season?

A) Darryl Sittler   B) Doug Gilmour
C) Mats Sundin   D) Rick Vaive

3 Who is the only member of the New York Islanders to score five goals in a game, twice in his career?

A) Mike Bossy   B) Pat LaFontaine
C) Piere Turgeon   D) Bryan Trottier

4 Who was the first goaltender in NHL history to win the Calder Memorial Trophy as the NHL's rookie of the year and the Vezina Trophy as the NHL's top netminder in the same season?

A) Tony Esposito   B) Ken Dryden
C) Glenn Hall   D) Terry Sawchuk

5 The Lester B. Pearson Award was first presented to the NHL's best player, as judged by his peers, in 1971. Who was the first player to win the Award three years in succession?

A) Bobby Orr   B) Guy Lafleur
C) Wayne Gretzky   D) Marcel Dionne

6 In which round of the 1989 NHL Entry Draft did the Detroit Red Wings select Nicklas Lidstrom?

A) 1st   B) 2nd
C) 3rd   D) 4th

7. The NHL record for the most losses by a goaltender in a single regular season stands at 48. Who holds this dubious record?

A) Eddie Johnston   B) Greg Millen

C) Al Rollins   D) Gary Smith

8 Who was the first player in NHL history to record at least 60 assists in a single season?

A) Stan Mikita   B) Gordie Howe

C) Jean Beliveau   D) Andy Bathgate

9 The Canadian Hockey League is recognized as the premier junior hockey league in the world. Who holds the record for the most career goals in CHL history, with 309?

A) Mario Lemieux   B) Guy Lafleur

C) Mike Bossy   D) Pat LaFontaine

10 Who is the only player to score 500 goals as a member of the Buffalo Sabres?

A) Dave Andreychuk   B) Richard Martin

C) Gilbert Perreault   D) Danny Gare

11 The NHL was formed in 1917. How many teams made up the league in 1917?

A) 3   B) 4

C) 5   D) 6

12 The Columbus Blue Jackets began NHL play in 2000. Who was the first captain in Blue Jacket history?

A) Ray Whitney   B) Luke Richardson

C) Geoff Sanderson   D) Lyle Odelein

1 Who was the first player in NHL history to appear in 200 Stanley Cup Playoff games during his career?

A) Raymond Bourque B) Mark Messier
C) Larry Robinson D) Guy Carbonneau

2 Wayne Gretzky registered 1,963 assists during his unmatched NHL career. Who stands second to Gretzky in career assists?

A) Ron Francis B) Mark Messier
C) Steve Yzerman D) Paul Coffey

3 Who is the only player in NHL history to record five assists in a single period of a regular season game?

A) Dale Hawerchuk B) Paul Kariya
C) Wayne Gretzky D) Bobby Orr

4 Who holds the NHL record for the most power-play goals in a single season?

A) Brett Hull B) Phil Esposito
C) Michel Goulet D) Tim Kerr

5 Since 1967, how many times has the NHL expanded its membership?

A) 7 B) 8
C) 9 D) 10

6 Name the first US-based team to be granted entry into the NHL.

A) New York Americans B) Boston Bruins
C) New York Rangers D) Chicago Blackhawks

7 Who is the only player in NHL history to be penalized over 700 minutes in his Stanley Cup Playoff career?

A) Dale Hunter   B) Claude Lemieux

C) Chris Chelios   D) Chris Nilan

8 Who has recorded the most career points among NHL defensemen in Stanley Cup Playoff history?

A) Al MacInnis   B) Paul Coffey

C) Raymond Bourque   D) Denis Potvin

9 The Minnesota Wild were awarded an NHL franchise to begin the 2000-01 season. Who did the Wild select with their first pick of the 2000 NHL Entry Draft?

A) Nick Schultz   B) Mikko Koivu

C) Pierre-Marc Bouchard   D) Marian Gaborik

10 Name the NHL goaltender who was known as 'The Hatchet Man'.

A) Ron Hextall   B) Ed Belfour

C) Glenn Resch   D) Billy Smith

11 Who was the first player in NHL history to score ten career regular season overtime goals?

A) Steve Thomas   B) Mario Lemieux

C) Theo Fleury   D) Sergei Federov

12 Who was the first defenseman in NHL history to record at least 30 points in a single Stanley Cup Playoff campaign?

A) Bobby Orr   B) Paul Coffey

C) Raymond Bourque   D) Denis Potvin

1   What is the maximum number of player inductees permitted in one year into the Hockey Hall of Fame?

A) 2   B) 3
C) 4   D) 5

2   The second edition of the international hockey tournament known as the Canada Cup took place in 1981. Who was voted the most valuable player in the 1981 Canada Cup?

A) Wayne Gretzky   B) Viacheslav Fetisov
C) Bryan Trottier   D) Vladislav Tretiak

3   Who was the first player in NHL history to record eight points in a single regular season game?

A) Elmer Lach   B) Maurice Richard
C) Bert Olmstead   D) Billy Taylor

4   How many times have the Chicago Blackhawks won the Stanley Cup?

A) 2   B) 3
C) 4   D) 5

5   The 1993-94 Detroit Red Wings had two players score at least 50 goals in the same season, for the only time in franchise history. Sergei Federov led the 1993-94 Red Wings with 56 goals. Who was the other Red Wing to score at least 50 goals that season?

A) John Ogrodnick   B) Steve Yzerman
C) Ray Sheppard   D) Brendan Shanahan

6   Who is the youngest player in NHL history to record at least 100 points in his rookie season?

A) Dale Hawerchuk   B) Sidney Crosby
C) Alexander Ovechkin   D) Mario Lemieux

7 Who was the first player in NHL history to be penalized at least 200 minutes in a single season?

A) Howie Young   B) Ted Lindsay

C) Reggie Fleming   D) Lou Fontinato

8 Who is the only coach in NHL history to be behind the bench for at least 700 regular season victories with one team?

A) Dick Irvin   B) Al Arbour

C) Scotty Bowman   D) Hector 'Toe' Blake

9 How did the Calgary Flames acquire the services of sniper Jarome Iginla in 1995?

A) via the NHL Entry Draft

B) via Restricted Free-Agency

C) via Trade

D) via Unrestricted Free-Agency

10 Who was the first defenseman to win the Conn Smythe Memorial Trophy as the most valuable player in the Stanley Cup Playoffs?

A) Jacques Laperriere   B) Serge Savard

C) Bobby Orr   D) Denis Potvin

11 Who has played the most NHL regular season games as a member of the New York Rangers?

A) Harry Howell   B) Brian Leetch

C) Rod Gilbert   D) Brad Park

12 In which year did the NHL make the wearing of helmets mandatory for players entering the league?

A) 1978-79   B) 1979-80

C) 1980-81   D) 1981-82

1 Who have the Toronto Maple Leafs played the most Stanley Cup Playoff Series against?

A) Boston Bruins   B) New York Rangers

C) Detroit Red Wings   D) Montreal Canadiens

2 Who was the first Russian-trained player to be selected first overall in the NHL Entry draft?

A) Alexander Ovechkin   B) Ilya Kovalchuk

C) Pavel Bure   D) Sergei Federov

3 Who is the only coach to win the Jack Adams Award as the NHL's coach of the year while a member of the Chicago Blackhawks?

A) Orval Tessier   B) Keith Magnuson

C) Mike Keenan   D) Bob Pulford

4 Which of the following players did not score at least 500 career NHL goals as a member of the Montreal Canadiens?

A) Guy Lafleur   B) Yvan Cournoyer

C) Maurice Richard   D) Jean Beliveau

5 In which year did the Quebec Nordiques relocate to Denver Colorado, thus becoming the Colorado Avalanche?

A) 1993   B) 1994

C) 1995   D) 1996

6 The record for the fastest two goals by one player in a Stanley Cup Playoff game stands at five seconds. Who holds this seemingly unbreakable record?

A) Dick Duff   B) Bob Gainey

C) Norm Ullman   D) Bernie Federko

7 The Montreal Canadiens have appeared in at least five consecutive Stanley Cup Finals twice in franchise history. Who is the only other NHL team to appear in five Stanley Cup Finals in succession?

A) Toronto Maple Leafs   B) Edmonton Oilers

C) Detroit Red Wings   D) New York Islanders

8 Who is the only player in NHL history to lead the league in goal scoring six consecutive times?

A) Wayne Gretzky   B) Bobby Hull

C) Mike Bossy   D) Phil Esposito

9 Who was the last player to be selected to the NHL's First All-Star Team despite being traded that season?

A) John LeClair   B) Jaromir Jagr

C) Wayne Gretzky   D) Chris Chelios

10 The Calgary Flames have won the Stanley Cup only once in franchise history. Who did the Flames defeat in the 1989 Stanley Cup Final to claim their only Championship?

A) Boston Bruins   B) Montreal Canadiens

C) Pittsburgh Penguins   D) Chicago Blackhawks

11 Who was the first goaltender to win the Lester B. Pearson Award as the NHL's outstanding player as voted by the NHL Player's Association?

A) Mike Liut   B) Patrick Roy

C) Ken Dryden   D) Tony Esposito

12 Name the last NHL team to see three members of the club selected to the NHL's First All-Star Team in the same season.

A) New Jersey Devils   B) Detroit Red Wings

C) Pittsburgh Penguins   D) Colorado Avalanche

1 Who played in the most regular season games in the short history of the World Hockey Association?

A) Ulf Nilsson   B) Marc Tardif

C) Andre Lacroix   D) Bobby Hull

2 Who was the first player in NHL history to receive over 1000 career penalty minutes?

A) Eddie Shore   B) Maurice Richard

C) Red Horner   D) Gus Mortson

3 Who was the first member of the New York Rangers to record at least 100 points in a single NHL season?

A) Jean Ratelle   B) Rod Gilbert

C) Brian Leetch   D) Pat LaFontaine

4 Name the Hockey Hall of Fame member who was given the nickname 'Secretary of Defense', during his playing days.

A) Tim Horton   B) Harry Howell

C) Larry Robinson D) Rod Langway

5 Who did the Florida Panthers try to draft in the 2003 NHL Entry Draft, even though he was ineligible for the 2003 Draft?

A) Sidney Crosby   B) Alexander Ovechkin

C) Evgeni Malkin   D) Alexander Radulov

6 With which NHL team did Darryl Sittler play the final game of his Hall of Fame career?

A) Philadelphia Flyers   B) Toronto Maple Leafs

C) Detroit Red Wings   D) Boston Bruins

7 Who was the first player in NHL history to win the Conn Smythe Memorial Trophy as the Stanley Cup Playoffs most valuable player, in consecutive seasons?

A) Bobby Orr   B) Wayne Gretzky

C) Mike Bossy   D) Bernie Parent

8 Who was the last player to record at least 90 assists in back to back NHL regular seasons?

A) Joe Thornton   B) Mario Lemieux

C) Adam Oates   D) Steve Yzerman

9 Which team holds the modern day record for the fewest losses in a single NHL regular season?

A) Montreal Canadiens   B) Philadelphia Flyers

C) Boston Bruins   D) Detroit Red Wings

10 Who is the only player in NHL history to record at least 100 points and accumulate over 100 penalty minutes in his rookie season?

A) Peter Stastny   B) Alexander Ovechkin

C) Sidney Crosby   D) Dale Hawerchuck

11 Who was the last member of the Montreal Canadiens to win the James Norris Trophy as the NHL's outstanding defenseman?

A) Larry Robinson   B) Rod Langway

C) Chris Chelios   D) Guy Lapointe

12 Who won the Lou Kaplan Trophy as the World Hockey Association's rookie of the year in 1979, the WHA's last year in existence?

A) Kent Nilsson   B) Wayne Gretzky

C) Rick Vaive   D) Rob Ramage

1   With which Quebec Major Junior Hockey League team did Hall of Fame member Mike Bossy play his major junior hockey?

A) Montreal Jr. Canadiens   B) Laval National

C) Hull Olympiques   D) Quebec Remparts

2   Who was the first non-North American player to be named captain of an NHL team?

A) Lars-Erik Sjoberg   B) Mats Sundin

C) Peter Stastny   D) Borje Salming

3   What was Gordie Howe's jersey number when he first entered the NHL in 1946?

A) 9   B) 15

C) 17   D) 19

4   Who was the first goaltender to win the Conn Smythe Memorial Trophy as the most valuable player in the Stanley Cup Playoffs?

A) Ken Dryden   B) Roger Crozier

C) Glenn Hall   D) Jacques Plante

5   Maurice Richard was one of only two Montreal Canadiens to record eight points in a single NHL regular season game. Who shares this Canadiens record with Richard?

A) Bert Olmstead   B) Jean Beliveau

C) Bobby Rousseau   D) Guy Lafleur

6   Who was the last player to be selected to the NHL's First All-Star Team in each of his first two seasons in the League?

A) Alexander Ovechkin   B) Raymond Bourque

C) Sidney Crosby   D) Wayne Gretzky

7 Who was the last player to record at least one point in 30 consecutive NHL regular season games?

A) Joe Thornton   B) Sidney Crosby

C) Joe Sakic   D) Mats Sundin

8 With which franchise did Doug Gilmour play the final game of his NHL career?

A) Toronto Maple Leafs   B) Montreal Canadiens

C) Chicago Blackhawks   D) New Jersey Devils

9 What was the nickname given to Philadelphia Flyers enforcer Dave Schultz?

A) Mad Dog   B) The Assassin

C) Bad Boy   D) The Hammer

10 Who holds the NHL single-season record for the most short-handed goals?

A) Wayne Gretzky   B) Mark Messier

C) Marcel Dionne   D) Mario Lemieux

11 Who did Alex Delvecchio replace as captain of the Detroit Red Wings to begin the 1962-63 NHL season?

A) Red Kelly   B) Ted Lindsay

C) Sid Abel   D) Gordie Howe

12 Who is the only player in NHL history to record four hat-tricks in a single Stanley Cup Playoff campaign?

A) Mike Bossy   B) Wayne Gretzky

C) Reggie Leach   D) Jari Kurri

1 Who was the last player to win the Lady Byng Memorial Trophy as the NHL's most gentlemanly player in consecutive seasons?

A) Ron Francis   B) Pavel Datsyuk
C) Paul Kariya   D) Patrik Elias

2 Bobby Hull scored 604 goals as a member of the Chicago Blackhawks. Who is the only other player to score at least 500 times as a member of the team?

A) Denis Savard   B) Jeremy Roenick
C) Stan Mikita   D) Dennis Hull

3 Who was the first European-trained player to be named captain of the Montreal Canadiens?

A) Mats Naslund   B) Andrei Markov
C) Saku Koivu   D) Alexei Kovalev

4 Who holds the NHL record for the most assists by a goaltender in a single regular season?

A) Grant Fuhr   B) Martin Brodeur
C) Ron Hextall   D) Ed Belfour

5 Who holds the Minnesota North Stars/Dallas Stars franchise record for the most points in a single regular season?

A) Bobby Smith   B) Mike Modano
C) Neal Broten   D) Dino Ciccarelli

6 Who captained the Swedish National Team to Olympic Gold in Turin, Italy in 2006?

A) Peter Forsberg   B) Mats Sundin
C) Daniel Alfredsson D) Nicklas Lidstrom

7 Which team holds the NHL record for the most consecutive road losses in a single season?

A) Washington Capitals   B) Winnipeg Jets

C) Ottawa Senators   D) San Jose Sharks

8 From which Western Hockey League team did the Montreal Canadiens draft goaltender Carey Price in the 2005 NHL Entry Draft?

A) Tri-City Americans

B) Prince Albert Raiders

C) Portland Winter Hawks

D) Spokane Chiefs

9 Who holds the NHL record for the most shutouts in a single regular season by a rookie goaltender?

A) Patrick Roy   B) Tony Esposito

C) Martin Brodeur   D) Dominik Hasek

10 In which year did the NHL introduce a lottery system to determine draft order in the NHL Entry Draft?

A) 2001   B) 2003

C) 2005   D) 2006

11 Who is the only player in history to register as many as five assists in a single NHL All-Star Game?

A) Joe Sakic   B) Mats Naslund

C) Wayne Gretzky   D) Vincent Damphousse

12 Who set an NHL modern-day record by scoring at least one goal in each of his first six games in the NHL?

A) Alexander Ovechkin   B) Teemu Selanne

C) Jordan Staal   D) Evgeni Malkin

1 Who holds the NHL record for the most career points in the All-Star Game among defensemen?

A) Bobby Orr   B) Paul Coffey

C) Raymond Bourque   D) Nicklas Lidstrom

2 Who is the only US-born defenseman to be selected first overall in the NHL's Entry Draft?

A) Erik Johnson   B) Gary Suter

C) Derian Hatcher   D) Brian Leetch

3 Who was the first player in NHL history to record at least 100 points in his rookie season and fail to win the Calder Memorial Trophy as the NHL's rookie of the year?

A) Joe Juneau   B) Sidney Crosby

C) Bryan Trottier   D) Barry Pederson

4 Who is the only player in NHL history to win the Art Ross Memorial Trophy as the NHL's leading scorer, despite being traded during that season?

A) Joe Thornton   B) Wayne Gretzky

C) Jaromir Jagr   D) Jean Ratelle

5 Name the netminder who holds the modern-day NHL record for the longest shutout streak during the regular season.

A) Bruce Gamble   B) Martin Brodeur

C) Ed Belfour   D) Brian Boucher

6 In which round of the 1999 NHL Entry Draft did the Detroit Red Wings select Henrik Zetterberg?

A) 1st   B) 3rd

C) 5th   D) 7th

7 Who won the inaugural World Cup of Hockey in 1996?

A) Canada   B) United States
C) Russia   D) Sweden

8 Who is the longest serving captain in the franchise history of the Edmonton Oilers?

A) Kelly Buchberger   B) Mark Messier
C) Wayne Gretzky   D) Jason Smith

9 The Buffalo Sabres have retired the jersey numbers of six players. Who is the only defenseman to have his number retired by the Sabres?

A) Phil Housley   B) Danny Gare
C) Tim Horton   D) Lindy Ruff

10 Whose name appears on the Stanley Cup the most times?

A) Henri Richard   B) Scotty Bowman
C) Jean Beliveau   D) Sam Pollock

11 Name the NHL team which boasts a record nine Calder Memorial Trophy winners.

A) Toronto Maple Leafs   B) Montreal Canadiens
C) Boston Bruins   D) Detroit Red Wings

12 Who is the only member of the Toronto maple leafs to win the Selke trophy as the NHL's top defensive forward

A) Alexander Mogilny   B) Doug Gilmour
C) Dave Keon   D) Dan Daoust

1 Who is the only player in hockey history to score at least 300 goals in both the NHL and the World Hockey Association?

A) Gordie Howe   B) Anders Hedberg
C) Derek Sanderson   D) Bobby Hull

2 Who was sometime referred to as 'The Russian Bobby Orr'?

A) Viacheslav Fetisov   B) Sergei Fedorov
C) Sergei Zubov   D) Alexander Yakushev

3 The NHL record for the most shots on goal by a rookie in a single season stands at 425. Who holds this record?

A) Alexander Ovechkin   B) Mike Bossy
C) Joe Nieuwendyk   D) Teemu Selanne

4 Who was the first defenseman in NHL history to score at least 20 goals in a single regular season?

A) Eddie Shore   B) Doug Harvey
C) Red Kelly   D) Frank Hollett

5 Who has recorded the most career assists as a member of the Detroit Red Wings?

A) Alex Delvecchio   B) Gordie Howe
C) Steve Yzerman   D) Ted Lindsay

6 Who is the only goaltender in NHL history to win at least 40 games in a season at least six times?

A) Terry Sawchuk   B) Patrick Roy
C) Martin Brodeur   D) Dominik Hasek

7 Who was the first hockey player to win the Lou Marsh Trophy as Canada's Athlete of the Year?

A) Gordie Howe   B) Howie Morenz

C) Maurice Richard   D) Bobby Hull

8 Who is the only defenseman to have his jersey number retired by the New York Rangers?

A) Harry Howell   B) Doug Harvey

C) Brian Leetch   D) Lou Fontinato

9 Who is the only member of the New York Islanders to win the Vezina Trophy as the NHL's top netminder?

A) Rick DiPietro   B) Glen Healy

C) Billy Smith   D) Chico Resch

10 Who was the last member of the Montreal Canadiens to score five goals in a single NHL game?

A) Guy Lafleur   B) Michael Ryder

C) Yvan Cournoyer   D) Bobby Rousseau

11 Which was the first US-based team to win the Memorial Cup, symbolizing major junior hockey supremacy?

A) Portland Winter Hawks   B) Plymouth Whalers

C) Tri-City Americans   D) Spokane Chiefs

12 Name the NHL team that won a league record 19 consecutive Stanley Cup Playoff Series?

A) Edmonton Oilers   B) New York Islanders

C) Pittsburgh Penguins   D) Montreal Canadiens

1   Who holds the NHL rookie record for the most consecutive games of recording at least one point?

A) Peter Stastny   B) Paul Stastny
C) Teemu Selanne   D) Wendel Clark

2   Who was the first Russian-born player to be inducted into the Hockey Hall of Fame?

A) Viacheslav Fetisov   B) Alexander Yakushev
C) Valeri Kharmalov   D) Vladislav Tretiak

3   Who is the longest serving head coach in the franchise history of the Toronto Maple Leafs?

A) Hap Day   B) Punch Imlach
C) Dick Irvin   D) Pat Quinn

4   Who is the only member of the Los Angeles Kings to score as many as 70 goals in a single NHL season?

A) Bernie Nicholls   B) Wayne Gretzky
C) Charlie Simmer   D) Luc Robitaille

5   Jean Beliveau broke into the NHL with the Montreal Canadiens in 1954. Who won the Calder Trophy as the NHL's rookie of the year that season?

A) Gump Worsley   B) Ed Litzenberger
C) Jean Beliveau   D) Camille Henry

6   Who holds the NHL record for the most years appearing in the Stanley Cup Playoffs?

A) Raymond Bourque   B) Chris Chelios
C) Larry Robinson   D) Mark Messier

7 Name the NHL enforcer who was often referred to as 'Knuckles'.

A) Stan Jonathan   B) Chris Nilan

C) John Ferguson   D) Bob Probert

8 Who is the only player to be named the Canadian Hockey League's Player of the Year, as the outstanding player in major junior hockey, two years in succession?

A) Mario Lemieux   B) Guy Lafleur

C) Sidney Crosby   D) Eric Lindros

9 Who finished second in the NHL's scoring race a record five times during his career?

A) Gordie Howe   B) Wayne Gretzky

C) Maurice Richard   D) Marcel Dionne

10 Who is the only player to win both the Lady Byng Memorial Trophy as the NHL's most gentlemanly player and the Paul Deveau Trophy as the WHA's most gentlemanly player in his career?

A) Wayne Gretzky   B) Dave Keon

C) Ron Francis   D) Mike Rogers

11 What is the name of the trophy awarded to the playoff champions of the American Hockey League?

A) Memorial Cup   B) Calder Cup

C) Campbell Trophy   D) American Cup

12 Which team boasts the most James Norris Trophy winners as the NHL's top defenseman?

A) Montreal Canadiens   B) Detroit Red Wings

C) Boston Bruins   D) Chicago Blackhawks

1   Name the Hockey Hall of Fame goaltender that has been given the nickname 'Mr. Zero'.

A) Frank Brimsek   B) Tony Esposito
C) Terry Sawchuk   D) Glenn Hall

2   Who is the only hockey player to win the Lou Marsh Trophy as Canada's Athlete of the Year more than once?

A) Bobby Orr   B) Gordie Howe
C) Guy Lafleur   D) Wayne Gretzky

3   Who was the last player to win the Art Ross Memorial Trophy as the NHL's leading scorer at least four consecutive times?

A) Wayne Gretzky   B) Mario Lemieux
C) Jaromir Jagr   D) Guy Lafleur

4   Who was the last member of the Toronto Maple Leafs to score at least five goals in a single NHL regular season game?

A) Dave Andreychuk B) Darryl Sittler
C) Ian Turnbull   D) Mats Sundin

5   With which Ontario Hockey League team did Steve Yzerman play his major junior hockey?

A) Kitchener Rangers B) Oshawa Generals
C) Belleville Bulls   D) Peterborough Petes

6   Who is the only goaltender to score a game-winning goal in NHL history?

A) Ron Hextall   B) Martin Brodeur
C) Ron Tugnutt   D) Roberto Luongo

7 Who is the only coach in NHL history to coach in five different decades?

A) Dick Irvin   B) Al Arbour

C) Scotty Bowman   D) Mike Keenan

8 Gordie Howe of the Detroit Red Wings won the Art Ross Trophy as the NHL's leading point producer six times during his career. Who is the only other member of the Red Wings to win the Art Ross Trophy?

A) Ted Lindsay   B) Steve Yzerman

C) Sergei Federov   D) Norm Ullman

9 Who was the last player to score four goals in a single period of an NHL game?

A) Dany Heatley   B) Mario Lemieux

C) Peter Bondra   D) Marian Gaborik

10 Who was the first United States Collegiate player to be selected first overall in the NHL Entry Draft?

A) Brian Lawton   B) Rick DiPietro

C) Mike Modano   D) Joe Murphy

11 Who are the only brothers to both be selected as the most valuable player in an NHL All-Star Game?

A) Frank and Peter Mahovlich

B) Bobby and Dennis Hull

C) Maurice and Henri Richard

D) Phil and Tony Esposito

12 Wayne Gretzky, Mario Lemieux and Mike Bossy all managed to score 500 NHL goals in fewer than 700 games. Who is the only other player to accomplish the feat?

A) Bobby Hull   B) Guy Lafleur

C) Jaromir Jagr   D) Brett Hull

1   Who holds the NHL record for the most power-play goals by a defenseman in a single regular season?

A) Dion Phaneuf   B) Sheldon Souray
C) Denis Potvin   D) Paul Coffey

2   Who finished second in voting for the Hart Memorial Trophy as the NHL's most valuable player a record four times during his career?

A) Jean Beliveau   B) Marcel Dionne
C) Bobby Hull   D) Phil Esposito

3   Who has recorded the most three or more goal games as a member of the Toronto Maple Leafs?

A) Charlie Conacher   B) Rick Vaive
C) Darryl Sittler   D) Mats Sundin

4   How many times did the Winnipeg Jets win the Avco Cup as Playoff Champions of the World Hockey Association?

A) 0   B) 1
C) 2   D) 3

5   Who was the first Russian-trained player to record at least 1000 points in his NHL career?

A) Alexander Mogilny   B) Sergei Fedorov
C) Pavel Bure   D) Igor Larianov

6   Who was the first team in NHL history to win at least 50 regular season games, four years in succession?

A) Montreal Canadiens   B) Edmonton Oilers
C) Detroit Red Wings   D) Boston Bruins

7 In which round of the 2000 NHL Entry Draft did the New York Rangers select netminder Henrik Lundqvist?

A) 3rd   B) 5th
C) 7th   D) 8th

8 Who was the first goaltender in NHL history to be named to the NHL's First All-Star Team four years in a row?

A) Bill Durnan   B) Jacques Plante
C) Turk Broda   D) Terry Sawchuk

9 Which Ontario Hockey League franchise has seen the most players selected in the history of the NHL Entry Draft?

A) Oshawa Generals   B) Kitchener Rangers
C) Ottawa 67s   D) Peterborough Petes

10 The NHL record for the longest drought between Stanley Cup Championships is 54 years. Which NHL team holds this record?

A) Detroit Red Wings   B) Chicago Blackhawks
C) Boston Bruins   D) New York Rangers

11 Who was the first player to record at least 30 points in a single Stanley Cup Playoff campaign?

A) Bryan Trottier   B) Mike Bossy
C) Phil Esposito   D) Frank Mahovlich

12 Who is the only player in NHL history to record at least two hat tricks with three different teams during Stanley Cup Playoff play?

A) Dino Ciccarelli   B) Wayne Gretzky
C) Mark Messier   D) Mike Gartner

1   In 1994, an NHL lockout of players resulted in the cancellation of 468 regular season games. How many games did each team play in this lockout shortened season?

A) 48 games   B) 44 games
C) 52 games   D) 56 games

2   The record for shutouts by a goaltender in a single NHL season is 22. Who holds this seemingly unbreakable record?

A) Terry Sawchuk   B) George Hainsworth
C) Tony Esposito   D) Jacques Plante

3   Who is the only forward to appear in the Stanley Cup Playoffs in at least 20 seasons?

A) Steve Yzerman   B) Mark Messier
C) Jean Beliveau   D) Gordie Howe

4   Who is the only defenseman in NHL history to win the Hart Memorial Trophy as the NHL's most valuable player four times during his career?

A) Doug Harvey   B) Bobby Orr
C) Raymond Bourque   D) Eddie Shore

5   Who is the only member of the Buffalo Sabres to win the Lady Byng Memorial Trophy as the NHL's most gentlemanly player?

A) Pat LaFontaine   B) Gilbert Perreault
C) Craig Ramsay   D) Pierre Turgeon

6   Who was the last member of the Boston Bruins to score at least 50 goals in a single regular season?

A) Joe Thornton   B) Phil Esposito
C) Cam Neely   D) Glen Murray

7 Who was the first European-trained player to score at least five times in a single NHL game?

A) Jari Kurri   B) Willy Lindstrom
C) Peter Bondra   D) Mats Sundin

8 Who coached the Montreal Canadiens to an NHL-record five consecutive Stanley Cup Championships?

A) Dick Irvin   B) Sam Pollock
C) Scotty Bowman   D) 'Toe' Blake

9 Who captained Canada to the Olympic Gold Medal in Salt Lake City, Utah in 2002?

A) Steve Yzerman   B) Mario Lemieux
C) Joe Sakic   D) Eric Lindros

10 Who was the first player in NHL history to play in 900 consecutive regular season games?

A) Gary Unger   B) Doug Jarvis
C) Steve Larmer   D) Stan Mikita

11 Who is the longest serving captain in the franchise history of the Boston Bruins?

A) Johnny Bucyk   B) Dit Clapper
C) Milt Schmidt   D) Raymond Bourque

12 On November 27th, 1960, Gordie Howe of the Detroit Red Wings became the first player in NHL history to record 1000 career points. Who was the next player to tally 1000 points in his career?

A) Bobby Hull   B) Ted Lindsay
C) Frank Mahovlich   D) Jean Beliveau

1 Which two teams participated in the 1987 Stanley Cup Playoff game that became known as 'Epic Easter'?

A) Rangers and Islanders

B) Islanders and Capitals

C) Bruins and Oilers

D) Flyers and Devils

2 Wayne Gretzky was the first player in NHL history to score at least 50 goals in a single season while still in his teens. Who is the only other player to score at least 50 times in a season while still a teenager?

A) Jimmy Carson   B) Alexander Ovechkin

C) Dale Hawerchuk   D) Sidney Crosby

3 In which round of the 1989 NHL Entry Draft did the Vancouver Canucks select Pavel Bure?

A) 2nd   B) 3rd

C) 5th   D) 6th

4 Who is the only player in NHL history to score at least one goal in ten consecutive Stanley Cup Playoff games?

A) Reggie Leach   B) Mike Bossy

C) Jari Kurri   D) Joe Sakic

5 The Montreal Canadiens have retired the jersey number of 14 different players. Name the only other NHL team to retire as many as ten player's sweater numbers.

A) Detroit Red Wings   B) Boston Bruins

C) Edmonton Oilers   D) Chicago Blackhawks

6 Who is the only member of the Calgary Flames to score five goals in a single NHL game?

A) Jarome Iginla   B) Theo Fleury

C) Joe Nieuwendyk   D) Lanny McDonald

7 The NHL record for the most points in a single season by a team failing to qualify for that season's playoffs is 95. Which team holds this record?

A) Montreal Canadiens   B) Colorado Avalanche

C) New Jersey Devils   D) San Jose Sharks

8 Who holds the NHL record for the most goals scored by a rookie in a single Stanley Cup Playoff campaign?

A) Mike Modano   B) Joe Nieuwendyk

C) Dino Ciccarelli   D) Claude Lemieux

9 From which Quebec Major Junior Hockey League team did the New York Islanders draft Roberto Luongo in the 1997 NHL Entry Draft?

A) Val d'or Foreurs

B) Acadie-Bathurst Titans

C) Rimouski Oceanic

D) Shawinigan Cataractes

10 Who was the last member of the Toronto Maple Leafs to lead the NHL in scoring?

A) Ted Kennedy   B) Charlie Conacher

C) Syl Apps   D) Gord Drillon

11 Who is the only US-born player to appear in over 1500 NHL regular season games?

A) Chris Chelios   B) Phil Housley

C) Mike Modano   D) Brian Leetch

12 Who was the last member of the Edmonton Oilers to record at least 100 points in a single NHL season?

A) Mark Messier   B) Doug Weight

C) Wayne Gretzky   D) Peter Klima

1 Which team boasts the most winners of the Lady Byng Trophy as the NHL's most gentlemanly player?

A) Toronto Maple Leafs   B) Boston Bruins

C) New York Rangers   D) Detroit Red Wings

2 Which of the following players failed to score at least 50 goals in his rookie NHL season?

A) Mike Bossy   B) Teemu Selanne

C) Alexander Ovechkin   D) Mario Lemieux

3 Who holds the Toronto Maple Leafs franchise record for the most shutouts in a single NHL season?

A) Turk Broda   B) Mike Palmateer

C) Johnny Bower   D) Harry Lumley

4 How many times have the New Jersey Devils won the Stanley Cup?

A) 1   B) 2

C) 3   D) 4

5 Who is the longest serving captain in the franchise history of the Chicago Blackhawks?

A) Chris Chelios   B) Stan Mikita

C) Dirk Graham   D) Pierre Pilote

6 Who was the last member of the Boston Bruins to be selected as the most valuable player in the NHL All-Star Game?

A) Bill Guerin   B) Raymond Bourque

C) Joe Thornton   D) Bobby Orr

7 Who has recorded the most career points in the Stanley Cup Playoffs, among European-trained players?

A) Jaromir Jagr   B) Sergei Fedorov
C) Peter Forsberg   D) Jari Kurri

8 Who was voted the most valuable player of the 1984 Canada Cup?

A) John Tonelli   B) Wayne Gretzky
C) Darryl Sittler   D) Mike Liut

9 In which round of the 1996 NHL Entry Draft did the Toronto Maple Leafs select defenseman Tomas Kaberle?

A) 2nd   B) 4th
C) 6th   D) 8th

10 Who holds the NHL record for the most consecutive career games played?

A) Andy Hebenton   B) Doug Jarvis
C) Steve Larmer   D) Garry Unger

11 Who holds the Montreal Canadiens franchise record for the most assists in a single NHL regular season?

A) Peter Mahovlich   B) Larry Robinson
C) Jacques Lemaire   D) Guy Lafleur

12 For which Quebec Major Junior Hockey League team did both Vincent Lecavalier and Brad Richards play their major junior hockey?

A) Hull Olympiques   B) Quebec Remparts
C) Rimouski Oceanic   D) Laval Titans

1 Who holds the NHL record for the most short-handed goals in a single season by a rookie?

A) Marcel Dionne   B) Jordan Staal
C) Jere Lehtonen   D) Mike Peca

2 Who is the only player in NHL history to score at least 50 goals in a season nine consecutive times?

A) Wayne Gretzky   B) Phil Esposito
C) Mario Lemieux   D) Mike Bossy

3 Who is the only member of the St. Louis Blues to score at least six goals in a single NHL game?

A) Brian Sutter   B) Bernie Federko
C) Red Berenson   D) Brett Hull

4 Who is the only player in history to lead the NHL in penalty minutes for eight years in succession?

A) Dave Williams   B) Red Horner
C) Eddie Shore   D) Dave Schultz

5 How many times did Wayne Gretzky record at least 200 points in a single NHL regular season?

A) 2   B) 3
C) 4   D) 5

6 Who is the only member of the Pittsburgh Penguins to win the James Norris Trophy as the NHL's outstanding defenseman?

A) Paul Coffey   B) Sergei Gonchar
C) Randy Carlyle   D) Larry Murphy

7 Who is the only member of the Detroit Red Wings to score at least 10 short-handed goals in a single NHL season?

A) Kris Draper   B) Sergei Fedorov

C) Marcel Dionne   D) Steve Yzerman

8 Who was the first NHL rookie defenseman to score at least 20 goals in a single regular season?

A) Barry Beck   B) Bobby Orr

C) Denis Potvin   D) Phil Housley

9 Who was the last member of the Montreal Canadiens to win the Calder Memorial Trophy as the NHL's top rookie?

A) Guy Lafleur   B) Mats Naslund

C) Patrick Roy   D) Ken Dryden

10 During the 1943-44 NHL season, the Montreal Canadiens famed 'Punch Line' was formed. Which of the following players was not a member of this prolific-scoring line?

A) Elmer Lach   B) 'Toe' Blake

C) Howie Morenz   D) Maurice Richard

11 Who is the only member of the Boston Bruins to record at least 100 points in a single season six consecutive times?

A) Phil Esposito   B) Bobby Orr

C) Rick Middleton   D) Raymond Bourque

12 In 2006-2007, Martin Brodeur of the New Jersey Devils established a new NHL record for victories by a goaltender in a single season with 48. Who held this record prior to Brodeur?

A) Terry Sawchuk   B) Martin Brodeur

C) Dominik Hasek   D) Bernie Parent

1 Who was the last member of the Toronto Maple Leafs to record at least 10 shutouts in a single NHL regular season?

A) Ed Belfour   B) Curtis Joseph
C) Felix Potvin   D) Andrew Raycroft

2 With which NHL franchise did sniper Brendan Shanahan begin his professional career?

A) New Jersey Devils   B) St. Louis Blues
C) Detroit Red Wings   D) Dallas Stars

3 How many different NHL teams did Roger Neilson coach during his lengthy coaching career?

A) 6   B) 7
C) 8   D) 9

4 Who is known as the 'Russian Rocket'?

A) Evgeni Malkin   B) Pavel Bure
C) Alexander Ovechkin   D) Ilya Kovalchuk

5 Name the two teams that participated in the only Stanley Cup Final that saw each and every game decided in overtime.

A) Toronto and Detroit   B) Montreal and Boston
C) Montreal and Toronto   D) Boston and St. Louis

6 The NHL record for short-handed goals by a team in a single regular season stands at 36. Which team holds this impressive record?

A) Detroit Red Wings   B) Edmonton Oilers
C) Pittsburgh Penguins   D) Dallas Stars

7 Who was the first goaltender to be selected the most valuable player in the NHL All-Star Game?

A) Terry Sawchuk   B) Johnny Bower

C) Bruce Gamble   D) Glenn Hall

8 Name the player that the Montreal Canadiens sought so frantically that they were prompted to purchase the entire Quebec Hockey League to obtain his services.

A) Jean Beliveau   B) Jacques Plante

C) Maurice Richard   D) Guy Lafleur

9 Who is the only member of the Boston Bruins to win the Frank Selke Trophy as the NHL's top defensive forward?

A) Steve Kasper   B) Ed Westfall

C) Craig Janney   D) Rick Middleton

10 How many different NHL teams did Paul Coffey play for during his Hall of Fame career?

A) 4   B) 6

C) 7   D) 9

11 Who was the last player to win the Frank Selke Trophy as the NHL's best defensive forward in consecutive seasons?

A) Sergei Fedorov   B) Rod Brind'amour

C) Guy Carbonneau   D) Jere Lehtinen

12 With which World Hockey Association franchise did Mark Messier begin his professional hockey career?

A) Hartford Whalers

B) Edmonton Oilers

C) Indianapolis Racers

D) Minnesota Fighting Saints

1   The Dallas Stars captured their first and only Stanley Cup in 1999. Who was the coach of the Stars in their Cup winning season?

A) Bob Gainey   B) Jacques Lemaire
C) Ron Wilson   D) Ken Hitchcock

2   Who was the first European-trained player to be selected first overall in the NHL's Entry Draft?

A) Alexei Yashin   B) Ilya Kovalchuk
C) Mats Sundin   D) Alexander Ovechkin

3   Name the player who has recorded the most NHL regular season victories among US-born goaltenders.

A) Mike Richter   B) John Vanbiesbrouck
C) Tom Barrasso   D) Frank Brimsek

4   For which team did the controversial Don Cherry play his only game in the NHL?

A) Toronto Maple Leafs   B) Boston Bruins
C) Chicago Blackhawks   D) New York Rangers

5   Who was the first NHL'er to appear on the cover of Sports Illustrated?

A) Maurice Richard   B) Jean Beliveau
C) Gordie Howe   D) Bobby Hull

6   Who holds the NHL record for the most consecutive complete games played by a goaltender?

A) Jacques Plante   B) Ed Giacomin
C) Glenn Hall   D) Terry Sawchuk

7 Who holds the Toronto Maple Leafs franchise record for the most career assists?

A) Mats Sundin   B) Darryl Sittler

C) Dave Keon   D) Borje Salming

8 Which of the following players was not a member of the Los Angeles Kings famed 'Triple Crown Line'?

A) Marcel Dionne   B) Charlie Simmer

C) Luc Robitaille   D) Dave Taylor

9 The 1992-93 NHL season produced a record number of 50 goalscorers. How many players scored at least 50 times during the 1992-93 season?

A) 14   B) 16

C) 18   D) 20

10 Who was the first player to score two short-handed goals in a single Stanley Cup Playoff game?

A) Claude Provost   B) Wayne Gretzky

C) Dave Keon   D) Bryan Trottier

11 How many different NHL teams did Al Arbour coach during his magnificent coaching career?

A) 1   B) 2

C) 3   D) 4

12 Who was the last player to score the Stanley Cup winning goal in overtime?

A) Brett Hull   B) Jason Arnott

C) Uwe Krupp   D) Mark Messier

1   Name the NHL goaltender that was often referred to as 'Apple Cheeks'.

A) Gerry Cheevers   B) Don Simmons
C) Harry Lumley   D) Charlie Hodge

2   Who is the longest serving captain in the franchise history of the New York Islanders?

A) Brent Sutter   B) Denis Potvin
C) Bryan Trottier   D) Pat Flatley

3   Wayne Gretzky and Mark Messier both recorded over 500 regular season points for two different teams during their Hall of Fame career's. Who is the only other player to accomplish this feat?

A) Paul Coffey   B) Brett Hull
C) Ron Francis   D) Jaromir Jagr

4   Who was the first member of the Pittsburgh Penguins to record at least 100 points in a single NHL regular season?

A) Mike Bullard   B) Jean Pronovost
C) Pierre Larouche   D) Mario Lemieux

5   Who holds the NHL record for the longest consecutive game point-streak in a single Stanley Cup Playoff campaign?

A) Wayne Gretzky   B) Guy Lafleur
C) Mario Lemieux   D) Bryan Trottier

6   Which nation won the World Junior Hockey Championships a record seven times in succession?

A) Sweden   B) Canada
C) Soviet Union   D) United States

7 Which is the only team in NHL history to have 11 players score at least 20 goals in the same season?

A) Boston Bruins B) Montreal Canadiens
C) Edmonton Oilers D) Philadelphia Flyers

8 Who is the only man to have his name inscribed on the Stanley Cup as a player, coach and general manager?

A) 'Toe' Blake B) Milt Schmidt
C) Scotty Bowman D) Jack Adams

9 Who is the only player in NHL history to record three five goal games in a single NHL regular season?

A) Joe Malone B) Newsy Lalonde
C) Wayne Gretzky D) Mario Lemieux

10 Who is the only member of the New Jersey Devils to win the James Norris Trophy as the NHL's best defenseman?

A) Viacheslav Fetisov B) Brian Rafalski
C) Scott Stevens D) Scott Niedermayer

11 Who holds the Vancouver Canucks franchise record for the most points in a single NHL season?

A) Pavel Bure B) Markus Naslund
C) Trevor Linden D) Todd Bertuzzi

12 Name the two cities that were granted NHL franchises to begin the 1970-71 season.

A) Atlanta and Buffalo
B) Buffalo and Vancouver
C) Cleveland and Atlanta
D) Kansas City and Denver

1   Who was the last team to win the Memorial Cup in back-to-back seasons?

A) Kamloops Blazers
B) London Knights
C) Peterborough Petes
D) Brandon Wheat Kings

2   Who was the last member of the Montreal Canadiens to score at least 50 goals in a single NHL season?

A) Steve Shutt   B) Guy Lafleur
C) Mats Naslund   D) Stephane Richer

3   Who was the diminutive NHL forward who was often referred to as 'The Little Ball of Hate'?

A) Pat Verbeek   B) Ken Linseman
C) Dino Ciccarelli   D) Theo Fleury

4   Who was the last member of the Detroit Red Wings to win the Calder Memorial Trophy as the NHL's rookie of the year?

A) Roger Crozier   B) Marcel Dionne
C) Steve Yzerman   D) Pavel Datsyuk

5   Name the goaltender who created NHL history by shutting out a record 11 different teams in a single regular season.

A) Martin Brodeur   B) Dominik Hasek
C) Patrick Roy   D) Curtis Joseph

6   Who was the first NHL team to win the Stanley Cup, three years in succession?

A) Toronto Maple Leafs   B) Boston Bruins
C) Montreal Canadiens   D) Detroit Red Wings

7 Who was the first goaltender to have his jersey retired by an NHL team?

A) Jacques Plante   B) Glenn Hall

C) Terry Sawchuk   D) Bernie Parent

8 What was the name of the Calgary franchise that was a member of the World Hockey Association from 1975 until 1977?

A) Cannons   B) Cowboys

C) Mountaineers   D) Dinos

9 How many different teams did Adam Oates play for during his productive NHL career?

A) 5   B) 6

C) 7   D) 8

10 Who was the first player in NHL history to score at least 20 goals in a season for six different teams?

A) Ray Sheppard   B) Doug Gilmour

C) Mike Sillinger   D) Mike Gartner

11 Who has recorded the most points in a single NHL regular season among Sweden-trained players?

A) Peter Forsberg   B) Mats Sundin

C) Markus Naslund   D) Kent Nilsson

12 Who is the only coach to win the Jack Adams Award as the NHL's coach of the year on three different occasions?

A) Jacques Demers   B) Scotty Bowman

C) Fred Shero   D) Pat Burns

1 Major League pitcher Tom Glavine was selected 69th overall in the 1984 NHL Entry Draft. Which team selected Glavine with their 4th pick of this draft?

A) Los Angeles Kings
B) Minnesota North Stars
C) Washington Capitals
D) St. Louis Blues

2 Who has played in the most NHL All-Star games?

A) Wayne Gretzky   B) Raymond Bourque
C) Chris Chelios   D) Gordie Howe

3 Who succeeded George Armstrong as the captain of the Toronto Maple Leafs upon Armstrong's retirement at the conclusion of the 1970-71 season?

A) Norm Ullman   B) Tim Horton
C) Dave Keon   D) Darryl Sittler

4 How many different members of the Edmonton Oilers have won the Conn Smythe Memorial Trophy as the NHL's most valuable player in the Stanley Cup Playoffs?

A) 2   B) 3
C) 4   D) 5

5 Who is the youngest player in NHL history to participate in a regular season game?

A) Bep Guidolin   B) Bobby Orr
C) Harry Lumley   D) Sidney Crosby

6 Who was the last player to remain active in the NHL who was named to Team Canada for the 1972 Summit Series against the Russians?

A) Bobby Clarke   B) Gilbert Perreault
C) Tony Esposito   D) Marcel Dionne

7 Which of the following players did not record at least 1000 career NHL points as a member of the Chicago Blackhawks?

A) Stan Mikita   B) Jeremy Roenick
C) Bobby Hull   D) Denis Savard

8 The James Norris Trophy was first awarded to the NHL's top defenseman in 1954. How many different members of the Montreal Canadiens have won the Norris?

A) 4   B) 5
C) 6   D) 7

9 Against which goalkeeper did Steve Yzerman, Joe Mullen and Brendan Shanahan all score their 500th career NHL goal?

A) Dominik Hasek   B) Ed Belfour
C) Martin Brodeur   D) Patrick Roy

10 Which is the only team in NHL history to have two players score at least 70 goals in the same regular season?

A) Edmonton Oilers   B) Pittsburgh Penguins
C) Los Angeles Kings   D) Detroit Red Wings

11 Who is the only player in history to die as a direct result of an injury suffered during an NHL game?

A) Bill Barilko   B) Joe Hall
C) Bill Masterton   D) Howie Morenz

12 In which season did the NHL institute the two-referee system on a full-time basis?

A) 1995-1996   B) 1997-1998
C) 2000-2001   D) 2002-2003

1 Who is the only player to score over 400 NHL career goals as a member of the Philadelphia Flyers?

A) Brian Propp   B) Bobby Clarke

C) Bill Barber   D) Eric Lindros

2 Who was the first Commissioner of the NHL?

A) Gary Bettman   B) Gil Stein

C) John Ziegler   D) Clarence Campbell

3 Who was the first set of brothers in history to each play at least 1,000 career NHL games?

A) Duane and Darryl Sutter

B) Frank and Peter Mahovlich

C) Maurice and Henri Richard

D) Russ and Geoff Courtnall

4 Who holds the NHL record for the fastest three goals in a single game?

A) Max Bentley   B) Elmer Lach

C) Bill Mosienko   D) Frank Nighbor

5 Who was the first player in NHL history to record 100 points in a single season while playing on a last place team?

A) Joe Sakic   B) Teemu Selanne

C) Mike Bossy   D) Alexander Ovechkin

6 With which Ontario Hockey League team did Chris Pronger play his major junior hockey?

A) Kitchener Rangers   B) Sudbury Wolves

C) London Knights   D) Peterborough Petes

7 How many different members of the Chicago Blackhawks have won the Art Ross Trophy as the NHL's leading scorer, at least once?

A) 2   B) 3
C) 4   D) 5

8 Who is the only player in NHL history to score all of his team's goals in a single regular season game while scoring five times during the game?

A) Sergei Fedorov   B) Mario Lemieux
C) Wayne Gretzky   D) Ian Turnbull

9 The Vancouver Canucks franchise record for points by a player in as single regular season game stands at seven. Who holds this record?

A) Pavel Bure   B) Stan Smyl
C) Markus Naslund   D) Patrik Sundstrom

10 Who is the only coach in NHL history to win over 200 Stanley Cup Playoff games?

A) Al Arbour   B) Scotty Bowman
C) Pat Quinn   D) Dick Irvin

11 Jaromir Jagr was awarded the Art Ross Trophy in the strike-shortened 1994-95 season on the basis of more goals scored. Who tied Jagr in points in the 1994-95 season?

A) Eric Lindros   B) Wayne Gretzky
C) Adam Oates   D) Ron Francis

12 Who holds the World Hockey Association record for the most points in a single regular season game?

A) Marc Tardif   B) Mark Howe
C) Real Cloutier   D) Jim Harrison

1 Who was the last team to have two defensemen selected to the NHL's First All-Star Team, in the same season?

A) Detroit Red Wings   B) Chicago Blackhawks
C) Montreal Canadiens   D) New York Islanders

2 Gordie Howe was the first player in NHL history to score 600 goals in his career. Who was the next player to attain this lofty total?

A) Marcel Dionne   B) Phil Esposito
C) Bobby Hull   D) Mike Bossy

3 Who has recorded the most points in a single NHL regular season among European-trained players?

A) Jaromir Jagr   B) Alexander Mogilny
C) Teemu Selanne   D) Jari Kurri

4 Who is the only player in NHL history to win the Stanley Cup four times with two different teams?

A) Bert Olmstead   B) Frank Mahovlich
C) Dick Duff   D) Red Kelly

5 Which team did Dale Hawerchuk play for when he scored the 500th goal of his NHL career?

A) St. Louis Blues   B) Winnipeg Jets
C) Philadelphia Flyers   D) Buffalo Sabres

6 Wayne Gretzky recorded seven assists in games three times during his NHL career. Who is the only other player to assist on seven goals in a single NHL game?

A) Elmer Lach   B) Mario Lemieux
C) Mark Messier   D) Billy Taylor

7 Who was the first player in NHL history to win the Art Ross Trophy as the NHL's leading scorer for four seasons in succession?

A) Stan Mikita   B) Gordie Howe

C) Phil Esposito   D) Guy Lafleur

8 Who is the only member of the Ottawa Senators to win the Calder Memorial Trophy as the NHL's rookie of the year?

A) Jason Spezza   B) Wade Redden

C) Daniel Alfredsson   D) Alexei Yashin

9 Who was the first goaltender to win the Calder Trophy as NHL rookie of the year and the Vezina Trophy as the league's top netminder in the same season?

A) Glenn Hall   B) Frank Brimsek

C) Terry Sawchuk   D) Mike Karakas

10 Who was the last member of the Chicago Blackhawks to record at least 100 points in a single NHL regular season?

A) Denis Savard   B) Jeremy Roenick

C) Steve Larmer   D) Eric Daze

11 How many different players have won the James Norris Trophy as the NHL's best defenseman while a member of the Boston Bruins?

A) 2   B) 3

C) 4   D) 5

12 For which Western Hockey League team did Jarome Iginla play his major junior hockey?

A) Kelowna Rockets   B) Kamloops Blazers

C) Red Deer Rebels   D) Vancouver Giants

1 Which coach has been in charge for more NHL All-Star Games than anyone else?

A) Al Arbour   B) Dick Irvin

C) Scotty Bowman   D) 'Toe' Blake

2 Name the NHL all-time great who was nicknamed 'The Big Bomber'.

A) Charlie Conacher   B) Eddie Shore

C) Syl Apps   D) Red Horner

3 Who was penalized a franchise record 1,777 minutes as a member of the Toronto Maple Leafs?

A) Dave Williams   B) Wendel Clark

C) Tim Horton   D) Tie Domi

4 Who was the inaugural winner of the Conn Smythe Memorial Trophy as the most valuable player in the Stanley Cup Playoffs?

A) Jean Beliveau   B) Dave Keon

C) Roger Crozier   D) Serge Savard

5 Who is the oldest player to be selected first overall in the NHL Entry Draft since the Draft's inception in 1963?

A) Rob Ramage   B) Bobby Smith

C) Guy Lafleur   D) Rick Pagnutti

6 For which team did Borje Salming play the final game of his NHL career?

A) Philadelphia Flyers   B) Toronto Maple Leafs

C) Boston Bruins   D) Detroit Red Wings

7 Who is the youngest player in NHL history to score three goals in a single regular season game?

A) Evgeni Malkin   B) Sidney Crosby

C) Mario Lemieux   D) Jordan Staal

8 At the conclusion of the 2007-08 NHL season, who has appeared in the most regular season games among European-trained players?

A) Jari Kurri   B) Jaromir Jagr

C) Teppo Numminen   D) Sergei Fedorov

9 Who was the last goaltender to appear in an NHL game without a mask?

A) Gump Worsley   B) Andy Brown

C) Glenn Hall   D) Cesare Maniago

10 Who was the first US-born player to score at least 50 goals in a single NHL regular season?

A) Joe Mullen   B) Bobby Carpenter

C) John LeClair   D) Mike Modano

11 Who is the only member of the St. Louis Blues to win the Calder Memorial Trophy as the NHL's rookie of the year?

A) Bernie Federko   B) Brian Sutter

C) Barrett Jackman   D) Brendan Shanahan

12 Which team did Paul Coffey play for when he recorded the 1000th point of his NHL career?

A) Detroit Red Wings   B) Edmonton Oilers

C) Boston Bruins   D) Pittsburgh Penguins

1 Which team did Adam Oates play for when he recorded the 1000th point of his NHL career?

A) Boston Bruins   B) Washington Capitals

C) St. Louis Blues   D) Detroit Red Wings

2 Who is the only defenseman in history to score an NHL record five times in a single regular season game?

A) Bobby Orr   B) Paul Coffey

C) Tom Bladon   D) Ian Turnbull

3 Which of the 'Original Six' arenas was the first to host an NHL game?

A) Boston Garden   B) Maple Leaf Gardens

C) Montreal Forum   D) Detroit Olympia

4 Who was the first goaltender to register over 400 regular season victories in the NHL?

A) Terry Sawchuk   B) Patrick Roy

C) Jacques Plante   D) Glenn Hall

5 Who was the first Russian-trained player to be selected first overall in the NHL Entry Draft?

A) Alexander Ovechkin   B) Alexei Yashin

C) Pavel Bure   D) Ilya Kovalchuk

6 Who was the last member of the New York Rangers to lead the NHL in goal scoring in a single season?

A) Lynn Patrick   B) Rod Gilbert

C) Andy Bathgate   D) Jaromir Jagr

7 Who has scored the most career goals in the Stanley Cup Finals?

A) Wayne Gretzky   B) Jean Beliveau

C) Mike Bossy   D) Maurice Richard

8 Who is the youngest goaltender to win the Conn Smythe Memorial Trophy as the most valuable player in the Stanley Cup Playoffs?

A) Ron Hextall   B) Patrick Roy

C) Roger Crozier   D) Bill Ranford

9 Who was the coach of the United States Olympic Team that captured Olympic Gold at the 1980 Winter Games in Lake Placid, New York?

A) Bob Johnson   B) Herb Brooks

C) Glen Sonmor   D) Pat Quinn

10 Who was the first member of the Toronto Maple Leafs to record at least 100 points in a single NHL regular season?

A) Frank Mahovlich   B) Doug Gilmour

C) Mats Sundin   D) Darryl Sittler

11 Who succeeded Steve Yzerman as the captain of the Detroit Red Wings to begin the 2005-06 NHL season?

A) Henrik Zetterberg   B) Kris Draper

C) Niklas Lidstrom   D) Chris Chelios

12 Who was the first player from a post-1967 expansion team to win the Art Ross Trophy as the NHL's leading scorer?

A) Bryan Trottier   B) Bobby Clarke

C) Mike Bossy   D) Wayne Gretzky

1 For which Quebec Major Junior Hockey League team did Mario Lemieux play his major junior hockey?

A) Laval Voisins   B) Montreal Jr. Canadiens

C) Quebec Remparts   D) Hull Olympiques

2 Who is the only member of the Dallas Stars to win the Conn Smythe Memorial Trophy as the most valuable player in the Stanley Cup Playoffs?

A) Ed Belfour   B) Joe Nieuwendyk

C) Mike Modano   D) Brett Hull

3 How many different NHL teams did Doug Gilmour play for during his illustrious career?

A) 3   B) 5

C) 7   D) 9

4 Which 'Original Six' franchise was moved to the NHL's Western Division from the Eastern Division to begin the 1970-71 season?

A) Chicago Blackhawks   B) Boston Bruins

C) Detroit Red Wings   D) Toronto Maple Leafs

5 Who was the first player in NHL history to score 500 regular season goals in his career?

A) Jean Beliveau   B) Gordie Howe

C) Maurice Richard   D) Bobby Hull

6 Which NHL team drafted Peter Forsberg in the first round of the 1991 NHL Entry Draft?

A) Quebec Nordiques   B) Winnipeg Jets

C) Philadelphia Flyers   D) Pittsburgh Penguins

7 Who was the first player in NHL history to win the Calder Memorial Trophy as the NHL's rookie of the year after already winning the Stanley Cup the previous season?

A) Danny Grant B) Ken Dryden
C) Tony Esposito D) Yvan Cournoyer

8 Who was the first coach to win the Jack Adams Award as the NHL's coach of the year with two different teams?

A) Pat Burns B) Pat Quinn
C) Scotty Bowman D) Marc Crawford

9 The first time that the NHL Entry Draft was held outside of Canada was in 1987. Which American city held the 1987 NHL Entry Draft?

A) New York B) Philadelphia
C) Detroit D) St. Louis

10 Who is the only member of the Los Angeles Kings to lead the NHL in goal scoring in a single regular season?

A) Wayne Gretzky B) Luc Robitaille
C) Bernie Nicholls D) Charlie Simmer

11 Name the two teams that failed to win the Stanley Cup during the 'Original Six' era (1942 to 1967).

A) New York and Boston
B) Chicago and Boston
C) New York and Chicago
D) Detroit and New York

12 Name the Hockey Hall of Fame member who was nicknamed 'Ukey'.

A) Bobby Bauer B) Vic Stasiuk
C) Terry Sawchuk D) Johnny Bucyk

1   For which Quebec Major Junior Hockey League team did Sidney Crosby play his major junior hockey?

    A) Rimouski Oceanic   B) Drummondville Rangers

    C) Victoriaville Tigres   D) Halifax Mooseheads

2   Who was the first European-trained player to be named to the NHL's First All-Star Team?

    A) Peter Forsberg   B) Peter Stastny

    C) Jari Kurri   D) Borje Salming

3   Who was the last player to lead the NHL in scoring while failing to average a point-a-game during the season?

    A) Howie Morenz   B) 'Toe' Blake

    C) Max Bentley   D) Ted Lindsay

4   The Philadelphia Flyers of the 1990s featured a lethal forward line known as the 'Legion of Doom'. Which of the following players was not a member of this outstanding forward line?

    A) Eric Lindros   B) Mikael Renberg

    C) Tim Kerr   D) John LeClair

5   Don Cherry began his NHL coaching career with the Boston Bruins. With which NHL franchise did he end it?

    A) Kansas City Scouts   B) Boston Bruins

    C) Colorado Rockies   D) Cleveland Barons

6   Who was the first player in NHL history to win the Hart Memorial Trophy as the NHL's most valuable player three years in a row?

    A) Bobby Orr   B) Gordie Howe

    C) Maurice Richard   D) Guy Lafleur

7 Who is the only player in NHL history to win the Hart Memorial Trophy as the NHL's most valuable player more than three seasons in succession?

A) Bobby Orr   B) Mario Lemieux

C) Gordie Howe   D) Wayne Gretzky

8 Who was the last NHL team to have centermen named to both the First and Second All-Star Team in the same season?

A) Montreal Canadiens   B) Detroit Red Wings

C) Edmonton Oilers   D) Pittsburgh Penguins

9 How many different players have scored at least 50 goals in a single NHL regular season as a member of the Calgary Flames?

A) 2   B) 4

C) 5   D) 7

10 Who was the last goaltender to play every minute of every game for an entire NHL regular season schedule?

A) Glenn Hall   B) Roger Crozier

C) Bernie Parent   D) Ed Johnston

11 Who was the first member of the Anaheim Ducks to record his 1000th NHL career point while playing for the Ducks?

A) Sergei Fedorov   B) Scott Niedermayer

C) Teemu Selanne   D) Paul Kariya

12 The original Ottawa Senators NHL franchise transferred to which US city to begin the 1934-35 season?

A) Pittsburgh   B) St. Louis

C) Philadelphia   D) Brooklyn

1 On February 6th, 1998, the Vancouver Canucks traded Trevor Linden to the New York Islanders. The Canucks acquired Todd Bertuzzi and one other player for Linden. Name him.

A) Markus Naslund   B) Bryan McCabe

C) Adrian Aucoin   D) Martin Gelinas

2 Who was the last defenseman to record at least 100 points in a single NHL regular season?

A) Raymond Bourque   B) Brian Leetch

C) Paul Coffey   D) Al MacInnis

3 How many different NHL teams did Scotty Bowman coach during his record breaking coaching career?

A) 3   B) 4

C) 5   D) 6

4 Who is the only player in NHL history to score all five of his team's goals in a single Stanley Cup Playoff game?

A) Mario Lemieux   B) Darryl Sittler

C) Reggie Leach   D) Maurice Richard

5 Who is the only goaltender to captain the Montreal Canadiens?

A) Bill Durnan   B) George Hainsworth

C) Jacques Plante   D) Patrick Roy

6 What was the name of the series between the Soviet Union and Team NHL that replaced the 1979 NHL All-Star game?

A) Summit Cup   B) International Cup

C) Challenge Cup   D) Canada Cup

7 Who was the first player in NHL history to participate in at least 100 Stanley Cup Playoff games?

A) Maurice Richard   B) Jean Beliveau

C) Turk Broda   D) Gordie Howe

8 Who was the first player in NHL history to record at least 90 points in a single NHL regular season?

A) Dickie Moore   B) Gordie Howe

C) Stan Mikita   D) Bobby Hull

9 How many different players have scored at least 50 goals in a single regular season while a member of the Toronto Maple Leafs?

A) 1   B) 2

C) 3   D) 4

10 Who was the last player in NHL history to receive over 400 minutes in penalties in a single regular season?

A) Bob Probert   B) Joe Kocur

C) Tie Domi   D) Mike Peluso

11 With which Western Hockey League team did Calgary Flames' Dion Phaneuf play his major junior hockey?

A) Kamloops Blazers   B) Calgary Hitmen

C) Red Deer Rebels   D) Vancouver Giants

12 Who was the last member of the Toronto Maple Leafs to be named most valuable player in the NHL All-Star game?

A) Frank Mahovlich   B) Doug Gimour

C) Rick Vaive   D) Vincent Damphousse

1 Who is the only player in NHL history to score his 500th career goal on a penalty shot?

A) Brett Hull
B) Mario Lemieux
C) Brendan Shanahan
D) Pierre Turgeon

2 To whom was Prime Minister Pierre Elliot Trudeau referring when he said: "Rarely has the career of an athlete been so exemplary"?

A) Bobby Orr
B) Jean Beliveau
C) Gordie Howe
D) Bobby Hull

3 Who is the only player in history to win the Lady Byng Memorial Trophy as the NHL's most gentlemanly player with three different teams?

A) Red Kelly
B) Ron Francis
C) Adam Oates
D) Wayne Gretzky

4 Who was the first team to win the Stanley Cup after being relocated from another city?

A) Calgary Flames
B) New Jersey Devils
C) Dallas Stars
D) Colorado Avalanche

5 Who is the only defenseman in NHL history to score more than 400 regular season goals in his career?

A) Raymond Bourque
B) Paul Coffey
C) Bobby Orr
D) Denis Potvin

6 Who is the only goaltender in NHL history to be selected to either the First or Second All-Star Team more than ten times?

A) Patrick Roy
B) Glenn Hall
C) Martin Brodeur
D) Jacques Plante

7 Wayne Gretzky scored 60 or more goals during an NHL regular season five times during his magnificent career. Who is the only other player to accomplish this feat?

A) Brett Hull   B) Mike Bossy

C) Mario Lemieux   D) Phil Esposito

8 The Montreal Canadiens of the 1970s featured a defense corp that became known as 'The Big Three'. Which of the following players was not recognized as a member of the Habs 'Big Three'?

A) Larry Robinson   B) Guy Lapointe

C) Rod Langway   D) Serge Savard

9 How many different players have won the Hart Memorial Trophy as the NHL's most valuable player as a member of the Pittsburgh Penguins?

A) 1   B) 2

C) 3   D) 4

10 Who scored the game-winning goals for Canada in both game six and seven of the 1972 'Summit Series' versus the Russians

A) Yvan Cournoyer   B) Ron Ellis

C) Phil Esposito   D) Paul Henderson

11 With which NHL team did Hall of Fame member Doug Harvey play the final game of his remarkable career?

A) Montreal Canadiens

B) St. Louis Blues

C) New York Rangers

D) Minnesota North Stars

12 Who is the only player in NHL history to win the Maurice 'Rocket' Richard Trophy as the NHL's leading goal scorer in consecutive seasons?

A) Pavel Bure   B) Jarome Iginla

C) Alexander Ovechkin   D) Teemu Selanne

1   Who is the only member of the Toronto Maple Leafs to win the Conn Smythe Memorial Trophy as the most valuable player in the Stanley Cup Playoffs?

     A) Terry Sawchuk   B) Johnny Bower

     C) Tim Horton   D) Dave Keon

2   How many times have the New York Rangers won the Stanley Cup?

     A) 2   B) 4

     C) 5   D) 7

3   Who was the first player in history to be selected first overall in the NHL Entry Draft to go on to win the Calder Memorial Trophy as the NHL's rookie of the year?

     A) Gilbert Perreault   B) Guy Lafleur

     C) Denis Potvin   D) Bobby Orr

4   The NHL record for shots on goal in a single regular season stands at 550. Who holds this record?

     A) Pavel Bure   B) Phil Esposito

     C) Alexander Ovechkin   D) Brett Hull

5   Who was the last player to score at least five goals in a single Stanley Cup Playoff game?

     A) Darryl Sittler   B) Joe Sakic

     C) Mario Lemieux   D) Daniel Alfredsson

6   Name the only major NHL award that the legendary Maurice Richard won during his illustrious career.

     A) Hart Trophy   B) Art Ross Trophy

     C) Lady Byng Trophy   D) Conn Smythe Trophy

7 Who is the oldest player to win the Conn Smythe Memorial Trophy as the NHL's most valuable player in the Stanley Cup Playoffs?

A) Niklas Lidstrom   B) Glenn Hall
C) Al MacInnis   D) Serge Savard

8 Gus Mortson and Jimmy Thomson formed an outstanding defense duo for the Toronto Maple Leafs during the 1940s. What was this defense duo's nickname?

A) 'The Leaf Brigade'
B) 'The Wall'
C) 'The Gold Dust Twins'
D) 'The Ministers of Defense'

9 Who are the only brothers to be selected in the first round of the NHL Entry Draft by the same team?

A) Daniel and Henrik Sedin
B) Rich and Ron Sutter
C) Ric and Barrett Jackman
D) Mario and Jocelyn Lemieux

10 Which team holds the NHL record for the most losses in a single regular season?

A) Washington Capitals   B) Ottawa Senators
C) Kansas City Scouts   D) San Jose Sharks

11 With which Ontario Hockey League franchise did Carolina Hurricanes' Eric Staal play his major junior hockey?

A) Windsor Spitfires   B) Kingston Frontenacs
C) Peterborough Petes   D) Sarnia Sting

12 Maurice 'Rocket' Richard was the first player in NHL history to score 50 goals in a single regular season. Who was next to accomplish this feat?

A) Bernie Geoffrion   B) Bobby Hull
C) Gordie Howe   D) Jean Beliveau

1 In which round of the 1998 NHL Entry Draft did the Detroit Red Wings select Pavel Datsyuk?

A) 2nd   B) 4th
C) 6th   D) 8th

2 Which was the last team to have linemates finish one-two-three in NHL scoring in a single regular season?

A) Edmonton Oilers   B) Boston Bruins
C) Pittsburgh Penguins   D) Detroit Red Wings

3 Who was the first European-trained NHL player to be inducted into the Hockey Hall of Fame?

A) Jari Kurri   B) Viacheslav Fetisov
C) Anders Hedberg   D) Borje Salming

4 The first NHL All-Star game was played on February 14th, 1934, at the fabled Maple Leaf Gardens. The game was held as a benefit for which NHL veteran?

A) 'Ace' Bailey   B) Syl Apps
C) Red Horner   D) 'Busher' Jackson

5 How many different members of the Washington Capitals scored at least 50 goals in a single NHL regular season?

A) 1   B) 3
C) 5   D) 7

6 Who is the only coach in NHL history to win two consecutive Stanley Cup titles with two different teams?

A) Scotty Bowman   B) Dick Irvin
C) Tommy Gorman   D) Billy Reay

7 Who was the last player to win both the Hart Memorial Trophy as the NHL's most valuable player and the Lady Byng Memorial Trophy as the league's most gentlemanly player in the same season?

A) Wayne Gretzky   B) Joe Sakic

C) Steve Yzerman   D) Sergei Fedorov

8 What was the name of the San Diego franchise that played in the World Hockey Association from 1974 until 1977?

A) Gulls   B) Stingers

C) Sharks   D) Mariners

9 Who is the only member of the New Jersey Devils to win the Frank J. Selke Trophy as the NHL's top defensive forward?

A) Patrik Elias   B) John Madden

C) Scott Gomez   D) Kirk Muller

10 In which season did the NHL reduce the number of games played by each team from 84 to 82?

A) 1990-1991   B) 1992-1993

C) 1995-1996   D) 2000-2001

11 Who holds the NHL record for the most short-handed goals by a defenseman in a single regular season?

A) Bobby Orr   B) Brian Leetch

C) Paul Coffey   D) Niklas Lidstrom

12 Who was the first player to win the James Norris Trophy as the NHL's best defenseman with two different teams?

A) Red Kelly   B) Larry Robinson

C) Pierre Pilote   D) Doug Harvey

1   How many times has the United States won the Olympic Gold Medal in hockey?

A) 1   B) 2
C) 3   D) 4

2   Who was the last member of the Montreal Canadiens to win the Calder Memorial Trophy as the NHL's rookie of the year?

A) Mats Naslund   B) Ken Dryden
C) Patrick Roy   D) Guy Lafleur

3   Which is the only team in NHL history to come back from a three games to one deficit in a Stanley Cup Playoff Series, to win, twice in the same season?

A) Pittsburgh Penguins   B) Toronto Maple Leafs
C) Vancouver Canucks   D) Minnesota Wild

4   Who is the only member of the Chicago Blackhawks to win the Art Ross Trophy as the NHL's leading scorer at least four times?

A) Max Bentley   B) Bobby Hull
C) Doug Bentley   D) Stan Mikita

5   Jacques Plante won the Stanley Cup six times while a member of the Montreal Canadiens. Who is the only other goaltender to play for six Stanley Cup winning teams?

A) Ken Dryden   B) Turk Broda
C) Grant Fuhr   D) Bill Durnan

6   Who holds the Calgary Flames franchise record for the most points in a single NHL regular season?

A) Theo Fleury   B) Jarome Iginla
C) Lanny McDonald   D) Kent Nilsson

7 How many different members of the Toronto Maple Leafs have won the James Norris Trophy as the NHL's best defenseman?

A) 0   B) 1
C) 2   D) 3

8 Who is the oldest player in NHL history to score 50 goals in a single regular season?

A) Gordie Howe   B) Wayne Gretzky
C) Steve Yzerman   D) Johnny Bucyk

9 Who was the last goaltender to win the Calder Memorial Trophy as the NHL's rookie of the year?

A) Evgeni Nabokov   B) Ed Belfour
C) Martin Brodeur   D) Andrew Raycroft

10 Who was the leading scorer at 2002 Winter Olympics in Salt Lake City, Utah?

A) Joe Sakic   B) Brett Hull
C) Mats Sundin   D) Mario Lemieux

11 Who was known simply as 'Mr. Goalie'?

A) Terry Sawchuk   B) Frank Brimsek
C) George Hainsworth   D) Glenn Hall

12 Who was the first player in NHL history to record 100 points in a single regular season?

A) Jean Beliveau   B) Phil Esposito
C) Bobby Hull   D) Gordie Howe

1 Who was the first player in NHL history to receive over 400 minutes in penalties in a single regular season?

A) Dave Williams　　B) Dave Schultz
C) Steve Durbano　　D) Keith Magnuson

2 With which Ontario Hockey League team did Eric Lindros play his major junior hockey?

A) Belleville Bulls

B) Ottawa 67s

C) Oshawa Generals

D) Sault Ste. Marie Greyhounds

3 In which year did the Stanley Cup come under the exclusive control of the NHL?

A) 1917　　B) 1926
C) 1931　　D) 1936

4 Who was the last member of the Detroit Red Wings to lead the NHL in goal scoring in a single regular season?

A) Gordie Howe　　B) Norm Ullman
C) Steve Yzerman　　D) Ted Lindsay

5 Who was the first rookie in NHL history to score five goals in a single regular season game?

A) Howie Meeker　　B) Bobby Rousseau
C) Gus Bodnar　　D) Mickey Redmond

6 Who was the first member of the Buffalo Sabres to score at least 50 goals in a single NHL regular season?

A) Richard Martin　　B) Danny Gare
C) Gilbert Perreault　　D) Rene Robert

7   Who was the first US-born player to be selected first overall in the NHL Entry Draft?

A) Joe Murphy   B) Jimmy Carson

C) Brian Lawton   D) Mike Modano

8   The San Jose Sharks became members of the NHL to begin the 1991-1992 season. Who was the first captain of the Sharks?

A) Doug Wilson   B) Pat Falloon

C) Bob Errey   D) Owen Nolan

9   Who was the only US-born player to lead the NHL in goal scoring in a single regular season?

A) Keith Tkachuk   B) John LeClair

C) Mike Modano   D) Jeremy Roenick

10   The Edmonton Oilers have had four players score 40 or more goals in the same regular season an amazing four times. Which NHL team is the only other team to boast four 40-goal men in the same regular season even once?

A) Boston Bruins   B) Calgary Flames

C) Pittsburgh Penguins   D) Los Angeles Kings

11   Who is the oldest goaltender to win the Calder Memorial Trophy as the NHL's rookie of the year?

A) Tony Esposito   B) Lorne Worsley

C) Ed Belfour   D) Evgeni Nabokov

12   The NHL Players Association was formed in 1967. Who was the first president of the NHLPA?

A) Carl Brewer   B) Bob Pulford

C) Doug Harvey   D) Ted Lindsay

1 Who was the first member of a 1967 expansion franchise to win the Hart Memorial Trophy as the NHL's most valuable player?

A) Bryan Trottier   B) Bernie Parent

C) Glenn Hall   D) Bobby Clarke

2 With which team did Hall of Fame goaltender Grant Fuhr play the final season of his stellar NHL career?

A) Buffalo Sabres   B) Toronto Maple Leafs

C) St. Louis Blues   D) Calgary Flames

3 Who is the only player in NHL history to record at least 1000 career points and accumulate more than 3000 career penalty minutes?

A) Wendel Clark   B) Brendan Shanahan

C) Dale Hunter   D) Mark Messier

4 Who has recorded the most career points in the World Junior Hockey Championships?

A) Evgeni Malkin   B) Peter Forsberg

C) Eric Lindros   D) Pavel Bure

5 Who was the last player from the 'Original Six' era to remain active in the NHL?

A) Dave Keon   B) Phil Esposito

C) Serge Savard   D) Wayne Cashman

6 Who was voted Canada's most outstanding hockey player of the first half of the 20th century?

A) Eddie Shore   B) Howie Morenz

C) Maurice Richard   D) Joe Malone

7 Who was the last member of the Detroit Red Wings to win the Art Ross Memorial Trophy as the NHL's leading point producer?

A) Steve Yzerman   B) Ted Lindsay

C) Gordie Howe   D) Henrik Zetterberg

8 How many times did Mike Bossy of the New York Islanders lead the NHL in goal scoring?

A) 0   B) 1

C) 2   D) 4

9 Which of the following players has not had his jersey number retired by the Edmonton Oilers?

A) Glenn Anderson   B) Grant Fuhr

C) Al Hamilton   D) Jari Kurri

10 Who served as team captain of the United Stares Olympic Hockey Team at the 1998, 2002 and 2006 Winter Olympic Games?

A) Brian Leetch   B) Chris Chelios

C) Jeremy Roenick   D) Keith Tkachuk

11 Who was the last member of the Toronto Maple Leafs to win the Hart Memorial Trophy as the NHL's most valuable player?

A) Frank Mahovlich   B) Ted Kennedy

C) Syl Apps   D) Darryl Sittler

12 Who was the last player to play in an NHL game without a helmet?

A) Guy Lafleur   B) Rick Middleton

C) Craig MacTavish   D) Al Secord

1 What is the name of the award presented annually to the best defenseman in the American Hockey League?

A) Doug Harvey Award   B) Don Cherry Award
C) Bobby Orr Award   D) Eddie Shore Award

2 Who is the only player in NHL history to average over two assists per game for an entire regular season?

A) Mario Lemieux   B) Wayne Gretzky
C) Herb Cain   D) Bobby Orr

3 Which NHL team was the last to have two players score four goals apiece in the same regular season game?

A) New Jersey Devils   B) Edmonton Oilers
C) Pittsburgh Penguins   D) Ottawa Senators

4 How old must a player be to be eligible for the Calder Memorial Trophy as the NHL's rookie of the year?

A) 22 or under   B) 24 or under
C) 26 or under   D) 30 or under

5 Who was the first hockey player to be named 'Sportsman of the Year' by Sports Illustrated Magazine?

A) Wayne Gretzky   B) Jean Beliveau
C) Gordie Howe   D) Bobby Orr

6 How many different players have won the Conn Smythe Memorial Trophy as the most valuable player in the Stanley Cup Playoffs while a member of the Philadelphia Flyers?

A) 1   B) 2
C) 3   D) 4

7 Who was the first European-trained player to score at least 50 goals in a single NHL regular season?

A) Jari Kurri   B) Peter Stastny
C) Kent Nilsson   D) Hakan Loob

8 Who was the last player to score five goals in a single NHL regular season game while in his rookie year in the NHL?

A) Michel Goulet   B) Anton Stastny
C) Don Murdoch   D) Alexander Ovechkin

9 Who was the first player in NHL history to receive a salary of over 10 million dollars for a single season?

A) Joe Sakic   B) Wayne Gretzky
C) Eric Lindros   D) Mario Lemieux

10 Who was the first player in history to win the Hart Memorial Trophy as the NHL's most valuable player in consecutive seasons?

A) Gordie Howe   B) Bobby Hull
C) Howie Morenz   D) Eddie Shore

11 Who is the only player in hockey history to win both the Hobey Baker Memorial Award as the NCAA's outstanding player and the Calder Memorial Trophy as the NHL's rookie of the year?

A) Chris Drury   B) Paul Kariya
C) Ed Belfour   D) Joe Nieuwendyk

12 Name the Hockey Hall of Fame member who was known as 'Old Boot Nose' during his NHL career.

A) Milt Schmidt   B) John Ferguson
C) Leo Boivin   D) Sid Abel

1 Name the netminder who recorded the most career shutouts in the short history of the World Hockey Association.

A) Gerry Cheevers   B) Ernie Wakely

C) John Garrett   D) Joe Junkin

2 The Montreal Canadiens have won the Stanley Cup four or more consecutive times on two separate occasions. Who is the only other team to win the Stanley Cup four years in succession?

A) New York Islanders   B) Detroit Red Wings

C) Toronto Maple Leafs   D) Edmonton Oilers

3 Who is the only player to participate in over 1000 NHL games as a member of the Edmonton Oilers?

A) Mark Messier   B) Esa Tikkanen

C) Kevin Lowe   D) Charlie Huddy

4 Who is the only player in NHL history to score four game-winning goals in a single Stanley Cup Playoff Series?

A) Jari Kurri   B) Joe Sakic

C) Darryl Evans   D) Mike Bossy

5 Who was the first member of the Philadelphia Flyers to have his jersey number retired by the team?

A) Bernie Parent   B) Barry Ashbee

C) Bill Barber   D) Bobby Clarke

6 Who is the only player to win the Les Cunningham Award as the most valuable player in the American Hockey League three years in a row?

A) Doug Gibson   B) Paul Gardner

C) Fred Glover   D) Johnny Bower

7 Which team was the first in NHL history to record at least 100 points in a single regular season?

A) Boston Bruins   B) Montreal Canadiens
C) Detroit Red Wings   D) Toronto Maple Leafs

8 On March 14th. 1986, Paul Coffey of the Edmonton Oilers recorded eight points in a single game to tie the NHL record for points in a single game by a defenseman. With whom does Coffey share this record?

A) Bobby Orr   B) Tom Bladon
C) Ian Turnbull   D) Pierre Pilote

9 Who was the last player to lead the NHL in post-season scoring even though his team failed to qualify for the Stanley Cup Final?

A) Peter Forsberg   B) Doug Gilmour
C) Phil Esposito   D) Joe Sakic

10 Who is the only member of the Los Angeles Kings to win the Hart Memorial Trophy as the NHL's most valuable player?

A) Wayne Gretzky   B) Rob Blake
C) Marcel Dionne   D) Rogie Vachon

11 Who is the longest serving European-born captain in NHL history?

A) Markus Naslund   B) Saku Koivu
C) Peter Stastny   D) Mats Sundin

12 With which Western Hockey League team did Scott Niedermayer play his major junior hockey?

A) Kelowna Rockets   B) Kamloops Blazers
C) Prince Albert Raiders   D) Regina Pats

1 Which NHL team has seen a record 42 of its players enshrined in the Hockey Hall of Fame?

A) Toronto Maple Leafs   B) Detroit Red Wings

C) Boston Bruins   D) Montreal Canadiens

2 Wayne Gretzky's younger brother Brent played a total of 13 games in the NHL. For which team did Brent suit up for, for all 13?

A) Hartford Whalers   B) Florida Panthers

C) New York Islanders   D) Tampa Bay Lightning

3 Who is the youngest goaltender to win the Calder Memorial Trophy as the NHL's rookie of the year?

A) Tom Barrasso   B) Martin Brodeur

C) Roger Crozier   D) Patrick Roy

4 During the 1960s, the Chicago Blackhawks featured a fabulous forward line known as 'The Scooter Line'. Which of the following players was not a member of this dynamic line?

A) Doug Mohns   B) Chico Maki

C) Stan Mikta   D) Ken Wharram

5 How many different teams did Wendel Clark play for during his NHL career?

A) 4   B) 5

C) 6   D) 7

6 In which season did the NHL introduce a five-minute sudden-death overtime in regular season games?

A) 1983-1984   B) 1988-1989

C) 1993-1994   D) 1998-1999

7 Frank Mahovlich and Pat Stapleton played for Canada in both the 1972 and 1974 'Summit Series' against the Russians. Who was the only other player to represent Canada in both series?

A) J.P. Parise   B) Bill White

C) Paul Henderson   D) Bobby Hull

8 Who is the only player in NHL history to score more than 10 short-handed goals in a regular season, twice in his career?

A) Mario Lemieux   B) Wayne Gretzky

C) Marcel Dionne   D) Dave Keon

9 Who is the only member of the Ottawa Senators to score at least 50 goals in consecutive NHL regular seasons?

A) Jason Spezza   B) Marian Hossa

C) Dany Heatley   D) Daniel Alfedsson

10 Who was the first US-born player to score 500 career goals in the NHL?

A) Jeremy Roenick   B) Mike Modano

C) Joe Mullen   D) John LeClair

11 Who was the last NHL rookie to win the Conn Smythe Memorial Trophy as the most valuable player in the Stanley Cup Playoffs?

A) Patrick Roy   B) Brad Richards

C) Eric Staal   D) Cam Ward

12 Name the two teams that took part in the famous 'Fog Game' that took place during the 1974-1975 Stanley Cup Playoffs.

A) Philadelphia and Buffalo

B) Montreal and Boston

C) Chicago and Buffalo

D) Boston and Philadelphia

1 Who coached the Edmonton Oilers to their four Stanley Cup Championships during the 1980s?

A) John Muckler   B) Kevin Lowe

C) Ted Green   D) Glen Sather

2 Who was the last player to record at least 90 assists in back-to-back NHL regular seasons?

A) Sidney Crosby   B) Wayne Gretzky

C) Joe Thornton   D) Marc Savard

3 How many times did Wayne Gretzky lead the NHL in goal scoring during the regular season?

A) 4   B) 5

C) 7   D) 8

4 Name the Hall of Fame broadcaster who made the phrase 'He shoots, he scores' famous.

A) Foster Hewitt   B) Danny Gallivan

C) Bill Hewitt   D) Dan Kelly

5 Who is the only player in history to win four major NHL awards in a single season?

A) Wayne Gretzky   B) Sidney Crosby

C) Bobby Orr   D) Stan Mikita

6 On July 25th, 1995, the Hartford Whalers traded defenseman Chris Pronger to the St. Louis Blues. Whom did the Whalers receive in exchange for Pronger?

A) Brendan Shanahan   B) Scott Stevens

C) Brett Hull   D) Adam Oates

7 How many different members of the Detroit Red Wings have won the Art Ross Memorial Trophy as the leading scorer in the NHL?

A) 1   B) 2

C) 4   D) 5

8 Who was named the most valuable player in hockey at the 2006 Winter Olympics in Turin, Italy?

A) Antero Nittymaki   B) Peter Forsberg

C) Teemu Selanne   D) Mats Sundin

9 Who is the only player in NHL history to play in the Stanley Cup Finals ten times and come away on the winning side in all ten?

A) Henri Richard   B) Yvan Cournoyer

C) Jean Beliveau   D) Serge Savard

10 Who is the only goaltender in history to win the Hart Memorial Trophy as the NHL's most valuable player despite the fact that his team finished in the basement of the NHL that season?

A) Glenn Hall   B) Ed Giacomin

C) Al Rollins   D) Gump Worsley

11 Who holds the NHL record for the most goals scored by a rookie defenseman in a single regular season?

A) Brian Leetch   B) Bobby Orr

C) Dion Phaneuf   D) Phil Housley

12 Who was the first goaltender to win 400 or more games with one NHL team?

A) Ed Belfour   B) Tony Esposito

C) Martin Brodeur   D) Terry Sawchuk

1 Who played a team record 21 NHL seasons with the Toronto Maple Leafs?

A) Tim Horton   B) George Armstrong
C) Allan Stanley   D) Johnny Bower

2 Who holds the Montreal Canadiens franchise record for the most goals by a defenseman in a single NHL regular season?

A) Larry Robinson   B) Sheldon Souray
C) Guy Lapointe   D) Eric Desjardins

3 On February 7th, 1976, Darryl Sittler of the Toronto Maple Leafs established an NHL record by recording ten points in a single game. Name the goaltender Sittler victimized on this historic night.

A) Gerry Cheevers   B) Gilles Gilbert
C) Dave Reese   D) Bernie Parent

4 Who has played for the most different teams in NHL history?

A) Michel Petit   B) Paul Coffey
C) Cory Stillman   D) Mike Sillinger

5 How many times has Sweden captured the Olympic Gold Medal in hockey?

A) 0   B) 1
C) 2   D) 3

6 Who was known as 'Scarface'?

A) Ted Lindsay   B) Borje Salming
C) Bryan Watson   D) Lou Fontinato

7 Who is the only player in NHL history to finish in the top five scorers an incredible 20 seasons in succession?

A) Jean Beliveau   B) Gordie Howe

C) Wayne Gretzky   D) Ron Francis

8 Who is the only player in NHL history to score four or more goals in a Stanley Cup Playoff game, three times during his career?

A) Mario Lemieux   B) Jari Kurri

C) Maurice Richard   D) Wayne Gretzky

9 To whom was Bobby Orr referring when he said: "His head and shoulders go one way, his legs go the other way, and the puck is always doing something else."?

A) Peter Mahovlich   B) Gilbert Perreault

C) Jean Ratelle   D) Guy Lafleur

10 Who was the coach of the Chicago Blackhawks the last time they won the Stanley Cup?

A) Billy Reay   B) Tommy Ivan

C) Rudy Pilous   D) Tommy Gorman

11 Name the first player in history to win the Lester B. Pearson Award as the NHL's outstanding player, as voted by the NHL's Players Association, with two different teams?

A) Brett Hull   B) Wayne Gretzky

C) Phil Esposito   D) Mark Messier

12 Name the veteran of 20 NHL seasons who was known around the league as 'Stumpy'.

A) Keith Acton   B) John MacKenzie

C) Steve Thomas   D) Cliff Ronning

1 Who was the last goaltender from the 'Original Six' era to remain active in the NHL?

A) Gerry Cheevers   B) Gilles Meloche

C) Bernie Parent   D) Rogatien Vachon

2 Who was the first European-trained player to win the Hart Memorial Trophy as the NHL's most valuable player?

A) Peter Forsberg   B) Nicklas Lidstrom

C) Sergei Fedorov   D) Jaromir Jagr

3 Four World Hockey Association franchises joined the NHL to begin the 1979-1980 season. Who was the first of these teams to relocate to another city?

A) Quebec Nordiques   B) Winnipeg Jets

C) Hartford Whalers   D) Edmonton Oilers

4 Who was the first member of the New York Islanders to have his sweater number retired by the franchise?

A) Billy Smith   B) Mike Bossy

C) Denis Potvin   D) Bob Nystrom

5 The fastest overtime goal in a Stanley Cup playoff was scored at the nine second mark of the first overtime period. Who scored this record-setting overtime goal?

A) Brian Skrudlund   B) Claude Lemieux

C) Theo Fleury   D) Doug Gilmour

6 Who were the first brothers to be selected to the NHL First All-Star Team in the same season?

A) Bill and Bun Cook

B) Lionel and Charlie Conacher

C) Doug and Max Bentley

D) Tony and Phil Esposito

7 Who was the last goaltender to be named the most valuable player of the NHL All-Star game?

A) Mike Richter   B) Martin Brodeur

C) Patrick Roy   D) Curtis Joseph

8 Name the American University that both Ken Dryden and Joe Nieuwendyk played their NCAA hockey prior to making their NHL debut.

A) Princeton   B) Harvard

C) Michigan   D) Cornell

9 From 1955 until 1962 Doug Harvey captured the James Norris Trophy as the NHL's top defenseman seven times in eight years. Who won the Norris Trophy in 1959, to interrupt Harvey's dominance of the award?

A) Red Kelly   B) Pierre Pilote

C) Tim Horton   D) Tom Johnson

10 Who won the Stanley Cup in 1927, the first year that the NHL assumed control of the Stanley Cup competition?

A) Montreal Canadiens   B) Boston Bruins

C) Ottawa Senators   D) Montreal Maroons

11 Who was voted the most valuable player of the 1976 Canada Cup?

A) Darryl Sittler   B) Vladislav Tretiak

C) Bobby Orr   D) Guy Lafleur

12 Which NHL team featured the 'Russian Five' during the 1990s?

A) San Jose Sharks   B) Detroit Red Wings

C) New Jersey Devils   D) New York Rangers

1 Who is the only player in NHL history to captain two different franchises to Stanley Cup Championships?

A) Ron Francis   B) Mark Messier

C) Jaromir Jagr   D) Bryan Trottier

2 Who were the first brothers to be selected in the first round of the NHL Entry Draft in the same year?

A) Ron and Rich Sutter

B) Daniel and Henrik Sedin

C) Dave and Dale Hunter

D) Jeff and Steve Larmer

3 Maurice 'Rocket' Richard finished his career in 1960 with an NHL record 82 goals in the Stanley Cup Playoffs. Who was the first player to surpass Richard's playoff goal total?

A) Jean Beliveau   B) Mike Bossy

C) Guy Lafleur   D) Bobby Hull

4 Who is the only player in NHL history to score an even strength, power-play, short-handed, penalty shot and empty-net goal in the same game?

A) Mario Lemieux   B) Mats Sundin

C) Mike Ricci   D) Sergei Fedorov

5 Who was the only player to play at least 20 NHL seasons with the Chicago Blackhawks?

A) Denis Savard   B) Stan Mikita

C) Eric Nesterenko   D) Bobby Hull

6 Wayne Gretzky won the Hart Memorial Trophy as the NHL's most valuable player nine times during his incomparable career. Who is the only other player to win the Hart as many as five times?

A) Gordie Howe   B) Bobby Orr

C) Mario Lemieux   D) Eddie Shore

7 Who is the only member of the Tampa Bay Lightning to win the Conn Smythe Memorial Trophy as the most valuable player in the Stanley Cup Playoffs?

A) Martin St. Louis   B) Nikolai Khabibulin

C) Vincent Lecavalier   D) Brad Richards

8 Who played a franchise record 884 consecutive NHL games with the Chicago Blackhawks?

A) Steve Larmer   B) Keith Magnuson

C) Elmer Vasko   D) Chris Chelios

9 Peter Stastny of the Quebec Nordiques set an NHL rookie record for assists with 70 during the 1980-81 season. Who would later record 70 helpers in a season to share the rookie record with Stastny?

A) Mario Lemieux   B) Joe Juneau

C) Sidney Crosby   D) Paul Kariya

10 Who was the first defenseman to record 1000 points during his NHL career?

A) Denis Potvin   B) Paul Coffey

C) Bobby Orr   D) Raymond Bourque

11 Who is the only non-goaltender to win the Conn Smythe Trophy as the most valuable player in the Stanley Cup Playoffs, while playing for the losing team in the Stanley Cup Final?

A) Claude Lemieux   B) Reggie Leach

C) Al MacInnis   D) Butch Goring

12 Who was known as the 'Stratford Streak'?

A) Syl Apps   B) Teeder Kennedy

C) Howie Morenz   D) Elmer Lach

1 Who is the only member of the Los Angeles Kings to record at least eight points in a single NHL regular season game?

A) Dave Taylor   B) Luc Robitaille
C) Marcel Dionne   D) Bernie Nicholls

2 Who was the first US-born player to record at least 100 points in a single NHL regular season?

A) Joe Mullen   B) Pat LaFontaine
C) Neal Broten   D) Doug Weight

3 Who is the only man to coach the Canadian Olympic Team in three different Winter Olympic Games?

A) Conn Smythe   B) Father David Bauer
C) Dave King   D) Pat Quinn

4 Name the siblings who between them have had their names inscribed on the Stanley Cup, as players, 19 times.

A) Doug and Max Bentley
B) Maurice and Henri Richard
C) Bill and Bun Cook
D) Frank and Peter Mahovlich

5 Who is the only member of the Atlanta Thrashers to record 100 points in a single NHL regular season?

A) Ilya Kovalchuk   B) Marc Savard
C) Dany Heatley   D) Marian Hossa

6 How many times did Mario Lemieux lead the NHL in goal scoring during his illustrious career?

A) 1   B) 3
C) 4   D) 6

7 Who was the first goaltender in NHL history to be credited with scoring a goal?

A) Ron Hextall   B) Billy Smith
C) Jacques Plante   D) Gilles Gilbert

8 The Edmonton Oilers won the Stanley Cup five times between 1984 and 1990. Which of the following players was not a member of all five Oiler Cup Championships?

A) Glenn Anderson   B) Grant Fuhr
C) Jari Kurri   D) Paul Coffey

9 Which team holds the NHL record for the most consecutive appearances in the Stanley Cup Finals?

A) Detroit Red Wings   B) Edmonton Oilers
C) Montreal Canadiens   D) Toronto Maple Leafs

10 Who is the only franchise in history to have a member of the team win the Calder Memorial Trophy as the NHL's rookie of the year three years in succession?

A) Toronto Maple Leafs   B) Pittsburgh Penguins
C) Boston Bruins   D) New Jersey Devils

11 Raymond Bourque of the Boston Bruins is one of only two defensemen in NHL history to score at least 20 goals in a season nine times during his career. Who shares this NHL record with Bourque?

A) Al MacInnis   B) Paul Coffey
C) Denis Potvin   D) Bobby Orr

12 Who was the last player to lead the NHL in goal scoring three consecutive times?

A) Brett Hull   B) Pavel Bure
C) Mario Lemieux   D) Jarome Iginla

1   Who was nicknamed 'Sudden Death' for his overtime scoring prowess during the 1939 Stanley Cup Playoffs?

A) Syd Howe   B) Nick Metz

C) Mel Hill   D) Woody Dumart

2   Who was the first member of the Detroit Red Wings to win the Lester B. Pearson Award as the best player in the NHL as judged by the NHL's Player Association?

A) Steve Yzerman   B) Gordie Howe

C) Marcel Dionne   D) Sergei Fedorov

3   Martin Brodeur and Roberto Luongo were two of the three goaltenders named to the 2006 Canadian Olympic Team. Who was the third goaltender that represented Canada at the 2006 Olympic Games?

A) Jose Theodore   B) Dan Cloutier

C) Ray Emery   D) Marty Turco

4   Who is the only member of the Calgary Flames to win the Conn Smythe Memorial Trophy as the most valuable player in the Stanley Cup Playoffs?

A) Lanny McDonald   B) Mike Vernon

C) Gary Roberts   D) Al MacInnis

5   Who is the only player to win the Frank J. Selke Trophy as the outstanding defensive forward in the NHL a record four times?

A) Kris Draper   B) Jere Lehtinen

C) Bob Gainey   D) Guy Carbonneau

6   Which major junior hockey team is the oldest continuously operating team in the Ontario Hockey League?

A) Oshawa Generals   B) Kitchener Rangers

C) Peterborough Petes   D) Ottawa 67s

7 Who was the first member of the Toronto Maple Leafs to score at least 50 goals in a single NHL regular season?

A) Dave Andreychuk   B) Rick Vaive

C) Lanny McDonald   D) Gary Leeman

8 Who was the last goaltender to win the Vezina Trophy as the NHL's top netminder and the Conn Smythe Memorial Trophy as the most valuable player in the Stanley Cup Playoffs, in the same season?

A) Grant Fuhr   B) Ron Hextall

C) Martin Brodeur   D) Patrick Roy

9 The NHL expanded from 22 to 24 teams in 1992. Which two cities were granted franchises to begin the 1992-93 season?

A) Ottawa and Tampa Bay

B) San Jose and Anaheim

C) Anaheim and Ottawa

D) Tampa Bay and San Jose

10 Johnny Bucyk, Bronco Horvath and Vic Stasiuk of the Boston Bruins formed a high-scoring forward line during the 1950s. By what nickname was this fabulous Bruin line known?

A) 'The Hot Line'   B) 'The Uke Line'

C) ' The Jobrovic Line'   D) 'The Assembly Line'

11 How many different players have won the Hart Memorial Trophy as members of the Montreal Canadiens?

A) 6   B) 8

C) 10   D) 12

12 Who was the first player in NHL history to record at least 100 assists in a single regular season?

A) Bobby Orr   B) Bobby Clarke

C) Wayne Gretzky   D) Bryan Trottier

1   Who is the oldest player to win the Calder Memorial Trophy as the NHL's rookie of the year?

A) Eric Vail   B) Peter Stastny

C) Sergei Makarov   D) Bobby Smith

2   Who is the only player in NHL history to be awarded two penalty shots in a single regular season game?

A) Andrew Ladd   B) Erik Cole

C) Eric Staal   D) Rod Brind'amour

3   Who is the youngest defenseman in NHL history to score at least 30 goals in a single regular season?

A) Phil Housley   B) Bobby Orr

C) Gary Suter   D) Doug Wilson

4   Name the only team in NHL history to score 400 or more goals in a single regular season.

A) Edmonton Oilers   B) Boston Bruins

C) Montreal Canadiens   D) Pittsburgh Penguins

5   Who was the first European-trained player to win most valuable player honors in the NHL All-Star Game?

A) Pavel Bure   B) Alexander Ovechkin

C) Teemu Selanne   D) Jari Kurri

6   Who is the only player in history to win the Art Ross Trophy as the leading scorer in the NHL while still a teenager?

A) Mario Lemieux   B) Sidney Crosby

C) Wayne Gretzky   D) Bobby Orr

7 Who is the only player in NHL history to win the Frank J. Selke Trophy as the top defensive forward and the Conn Smythe Trophy as the most valuable player in the Stanley Cup Playoffs in the same season?

A) Bob Gainey   B) Steve Yzerman

C) Bobby Clarke   D) Brad Richards

8 Wayne Gretzky scored at least 70 goals in an NHL season four times during his career. Who is the only other player in NHL history to score at least 70 times in three different seasons?

A) Brett Hull   B) Phil Esposito

C) Mario Lemieux   D) Teemu Selanne

9 How many times have the Peterborough Petes of the Ontario Hockey League won the Memorial Cup as champions of the Canadian Hockey League?

A) 0   B) 1

C) 3   D) 5

10 Who was the first member of the Detroit Red Wings to score at least 50 goals in a single NHL regular season?

A) Gordie Howe   B) Danny Grant

C) Marcel Dionne   D) Mickey Redmond

11 Who was named the tournament's most valuable player at the 2002 Winter Olympics in Salt Lake City, Utah?

A) Jarome Iginla   B) Joe Sakic

C) Steve Yzerman   D) Mario Lemieux

12 Who holds the NHL record for the longest undefeated streak by a goaltender during a single regular season?

A) Pete Peeters   B) Bernie Parent

C) Ken Dryden   D) Gerry Cheevers

1 Who was the last goaltender to be named to the NHL's First All-Star Team three consecutive times?

A) Patrick Roy
B) Martin Brodeur
C) Roberto Luongo
D) Dominik Hasek

2 The NHL franchise in Toronto became known as the Maple Leafs partway through the 1926-1927 season. What was the name of the Toronto team prior to being renamed the Maple Leafs?

A) St. Patricks
B) Shamrocks
C) Arenas
D) Blueshirts

3 Bobby Hull and Anders Hedberg formed two-thirds of undeniably the best forward line in the history of the World Hockey Association. Who was the third member of this fabulous trio?

A) Kent Nilsson
B) Ulf Nilsson
C) Andre Lacroix
D) Juha Widing

4 How many different members of the Boston Bruins have scored at least 50 goals in a single regular season?

A) 4
B) 5
C) 7
D) 8

5 The NHL record for the longest consecutive game winning streak by a team during a single regular season stands at 17 games. Which team holds this remarkable record?

A) Montreal Canadiens
B) Philadelphia Flyers
C) Pittsburgh Penguins
D) New York Islanders

6 Defensemen, Scott Stevens and Raymond Bourque both played over 1600 regular season NHL games during their careers. Who is the only other NHL defenseman to play 1600 regular season games?

A) Larry Murphy
B) Phil Housley
C) Al MacInnis
D) Chris Chelios

7 Which coach has led his teams to the most victories in Canadian Hockey League history?

A) Dick Todd   B) Roger Neilson
C) Brian Kilrea   D) Don Hay

8 Who was the last player to score four goals in the NHL All-Star game?

A) Dany Heatley   B) Brett Hull
C) Bill Guerin   D) Wayne Gretzky

9 First awarded in 1966, the Lester Patrick Trophy is awarded to honor a recipient's contribution to the game of hockey in the United States. Who was the first NHL player to receive this award?

A) Bobby Hull   B) Max Bentley
C) Gordie Howe   D) Bobby Orr

10 Who was the first team in NHL history to be on the losing end in the Stanley Cup Finals three years in succession?

A) Boston Bruins   B) Montreal Canadiens
C) Detroit Red Wings   D) Toronto Maple Leafs

11 Who was the last team in NHL history to lose in the Stanley Cup Finals three years in a row?

A) St. Louis Blues   B) Philadelphia Flyers
C) Toronto Maple Leafs   D) Pittsburgh Penguins

12 Who is the only player in NHL history to score over 500 career goals yet not record at least 1000 points during his NHL career?

A) Frank Mahovlich   B) Bobby Hull
C) Joe Mullen   D) Maurice Richard

1 Gordie Howe and Mario Lemieux are two of only three players in history to be active members of the NHL and honored members of the Hockey Hall of Fame at the same time. Who is the third member of this prestigious group?

A) Guy Lafleur   B) Wayne Gretzky

C) Eddie Shore   D) Bobby Orr

2 Who is the youngest player in history to be selected to the NHL's First All-Star Team?

A) Raymond Bourque   B) Alexander Ovechkin

C) Bobby Orr   D) Sidney Crosby

3 Who was the last NHL team to capture the Stanley Cup despite finishing the regular season with a sub .500 record?

A) Chicago Blackhawks   B) Toronto Maple Leafs

C) Carolina Hurricanes   D) Tampa Bay Lightning

4 The fifth and final installment of the Canada Cup was played in 1991. Canada defeated the United States 2-0 to claim the title. Who was named the most valuable player of the 1991 Canada Cup?

A) Mark Messier   B) Bill Ranford

C) Al MacInnis   D) Wayne Gretzky

5 Who is the only player in NHL history to lead the league in goals, assists, points and penalty minutes in the regular season at least once during his career?

A) Gordie Howe   B) Ted Lindsay

C) Maurice Richard   D) Jean Beliveau

6 Who is the only member of the Los Angeles Kings to win the Calder Memorial Trophy as the NHL's rookie of the year?

A) Bernie Nicholls   B) Rob Blake

C) Luc Robitaille   D) Anze Kopitar

7 Who is the only member of the Edmonton Oilers to score five goals in a single regular season game, more than once during his tenure with the Oilers?

A) Glenn Anderson   B) Mark Messier

C) Jari Kurri   D) Wayne Gretzky

8 Who was the first player to play at least 20 seasons in the NHL?

A) Eddie Shore   B) Dit Clapper

C) Turk Broda   D) Gordie Howe

9 Gordie Howe of the Detroit Red Wings was the first player in NHL history to record 1500 regular season points. Who was next to accomplish the feat?

A) Marcel Dionne   B) Stan Mikita

C) Phil Esposito   D) Bobby Hull

10 How many times was the legendary Frank 'King' Clancy named to the NHL's First All-Star Team as a defenseman?

A) 2   B) 3

C) 5   D) 6

11 Who is the only player in NHL history to win the Frank J. Selke Trophy as the NHL's top defensive forward with two different teams?

A) Rod Brind'amour   B) Mike Peca

C) Sergei Fedorov   D) Doug Jarvis

12 The nickname 'Moose' has been given to numerous players in the NHL? Which of the following players did not answer to the nickname 'Moose'?

A) Mark Messier   B) Andre Dupont

C) Elmer Vasko   D) Emile Bouchard

1 Who holds the single season NHL record for the most wins by a rookie netminder?

A) Ed Belfour   B) Martin Brodeur

C) Terry Sawchuk   D) Tom Barrasso

2 US-born Patrick Kane and James vanRiemsdyk were the first two players selected in the 2007 NHL Entry Draft, marking the first time in the Draft's history that Americans went one-two. Who was the first Canadian selected in the 2007 NHL Entry Draft?

A) Sam Gagner   B) Thomas Hickey

C) Kyle Turris   D) Karl Alzner

3 Who was the first player to win the Hart Memorial Trophy as the NHL's most valuable player and the Conn Smythe Memorial Trophy as the Stanley Cup Playoffs most valuable player, in the same season?

A) Jean Beliveau   B) Guy Lafleur

C) Bryan Trottier   D) Bobby Orr

4 Which trophy is awarded to the leading scorer in the Quebec Major Junior Hockey League?

A) Mario Lemieux Trophy B) Guy Lafleur Trophy

C) Jean Beliveau Trophy   D) Guy Rouleau Trophy

5 Bobby Hull is one of only two players to score 50 goals in a single season in both the NHL and the World Hockey Association. Who is the other?

A) Michel Goulet   B) Marc Tardif

C) Blaine Stoughton   D) Mark Howe

6 The 1963-1964 NHL First All-Star Team was dominated by the Chicago Blackhawks. Glenn Hall, Pierre Pilote, Bobby Hull, Stan Mikita and Ken Wharram were all selected to the team that season. Who was the only non-Blackhawk to be named to the NHL's First All-Star Team in 1963-1964?

A) Harry Howell   B) Bill Gadsby

C) Leo Boivin   D) Tim Horton

7 Name the stalwart NHL defenseman who was known as 'Snowshoes'.

A) Allan Stanley   B) J. C. Tremblay
C) Al Arbour   D) Lou Fontinato

8 Who was the first rookie in NHL history to score at least 50 goals in a single regular season?

A) Mike Bossy   B) Marcel Dionne
C) Richard Martin   D) Dale Hawerchuk

9 The Ottawa Senators have had the first overall pick in the NHL Entry Draft three times in the franchise's history. Which of the following players was not selected first overall in the Entry Draft by the Senators?

A) Chris Phillips   B) Alexandre Daigle
C) Bryan Berard   D) Jason Spezza

10 Raymond Bourque was selected to the NHL's First All-Star Team as a defenseman a record 13 times during his career. Who is the only other defenseman to be named to the First All-Star team as many as ten times?

A) Nicklas Lidstrom   B) Bobby Orr
C) Larry Robinson   D) Doug Harvey

11 Who is the NHL's all-time leading point producer among players who were draft eligible but undrafted by an NHL team?

A) Adam Oates   B) Steve Thomas
C) Dino Ciccarelli   D) Glenn Anderson

12 Frank Boucher won the Lady Byng Memorial Trophy as the NHL's most gentlemanly player seven times during the 1930s and 1940s. Who is the only other player in NHL history to win the Byng as many as five times?

A) Red Kelly   B) Wayne Gretzky
C) Dave Keon   D) Ron Francis

1 Who was the last player to score 50 goals in a NHL season in fewer than 50 games?

A) Alexander Mogilny   B) Brett Hull
C) Cam Neely   D) Mario Lemieux

2 Who was the first defenseman to win most valuable player honors in the NHL All-Star Game?

A) Bobby Orr   B) Pierre Pilote
C) Denis Potvin   D) Tim Horton

3 How many different players have won the James Norris Trophy as the NHL's best defenseman as a member of the Chicago Blackhawks?

A) 2   B) 3
C) 4   D) 5

4 Who is the only player to record at least 200 points in a regular season in major junior hockey's Western Hockey League?

A) Rob Brown   B) Doug Wickenheiser
C) Joe Sakic   D) Brian Propp

5 Who was the first player in NHL history to record over 30 points in a single Stanley Cup Playoff campaign?

A) Guy Lafleur   B) Mike Bossy
C) Bryan Trottier   D) Wayne Gretzky

6 The Detroit franchise in the NHL became known as the Red Wings to begin the 1932-1933 season. What was the name of the Detroit franchise immediately prior to becoming the Red Wings?

A) Falcons   B) Tigers
C) Cougars   D) Eagles

7 Who was the first defenseman in NHL history to record 500 regular season points during his career?

A) Doug Harvey   B) Bill Gadsby

C) Pierre Pilote   D) Bobby Orr

8 Who holds the NHL record for the fastest four goals by an individual in a single game?

A) Dany Heatley   B) Peter Bondra

C) Joe Nieuwendyk   D) Dennis Maruk

9 Gordie Howe and Mark Messier are two of only three players to play in over 1700 NHL regular season games. Who is the third member of the 1700 game club?

A) Scott Stevens   B) Larry Murphy

C) Ron Francis   D) Steve Yzerman

10 Who is the only member of the Vancouver Canucks to win the Calder Memorial Trophy as the NHL's rookie of the year?

A) Cam Neely   B) Trevor Linden

C) Stan Smyl   D) Pavel Bure

11 Who holds the record for the most game-winning goals in a single Stanley Cup Playoff campaign?

A) Maurice Richard   B) Mike Bossy

C) Brad Richards   D) Joe Sakic

12 Jose Theodore of the Montreal Canadiens won the Hart Memorial Trophy as the NHL's most valuable player in 2002, on the basis of more first place votes. Who tied Theodore in voting points yet lost the Hart in the closest vote in the Trophy's long history?

A) Vincent Lecavalier   B) Peter Forsberg

C) Joe Thornton   D) Jarome Iginla

1   How many times did Hall of Famer Scott Stevens win the James Norris Memorial Trophy as the NHL's top defenseman during his career?

A) 0   B) 1
C) 2   D) 3

2   Who is the only member of the Montreal Canadiens to lead the NHL in goal scoring in five different seasons?

A) Jean Beliveau   B) Bernie Geoffrion
C) Maurice Richard   D) Guy Lafleur

3   Who is the only forward in NHL history to win the Conn Smythe Memorial Trophy as the most valuable player in the Stanley Cup Playoffs in consecutive seasons?

A) Wayne Gretzky   B) Bobby Clarke
C) Mario Lemieux   D) Guy Lafleur

4   To whom was Chicago Blackhawks general manager Tommy Ivan referring when he said: "Break another seat in practice and it's coming out of your paycheck"?

A) Stan Mikta   B) Reggie Fleming
C) Bobby Hull   D) Dennis Hull

5   Who was the last goaltender named to the NHL's First All-Star Team in his rookie season in the league?

A) Martin Brodeur   B) Ed Belfour
C) Henrik Lundqvist   D) Dominik Hasek

6   Who is the only player in NHL history to win the Conn Smythe Memorial Trophy as the Stanley Cup Playoffs' most valuable player while playing for the losing team in the Stanley Cup Final before going on to play for a Stanley Cup winning team later in his career?

A) Reggie Leach   B) Mario Lemieux
C) Jean Sebastien Giguere   D) Martin Brodeur

7 Name the goaltender who lost an NHL-record 352 regular seasons games during his career.

A) Johnny Bower   B) Gump Worsley

C) Ed Giacomin   D) Rogatien Vachon

8 Who was the first player in NHL history to score at least 20 goals in a regular season for five different teams?

A) Mike Gartner   B) Paul Coffey

C) Andy Bathgate   D) Eddie Shack

9 In which round of the 1982 NHL Entry Draft was Doug Gilmour selected by the St. Louis Blues?

A) 2nd   B) 4th

C) 5th   D) 7th

10 Who was the first player to win an Olympic Gold Medal and a Stanley Cup Championship ring in the same year?

A) Ken Morrow   B) Dominik Hasek

C) Scott Niedermayer   D) Peter Forsberg

11 Doug Harvey won the James Norris Memorial Trophy six times as a member of the Montreal Canadiens. Who is the only other Habitant to win the Norris at least twice as a member of the club?

A) Larry Robinson   B) Chris Chelios

C) Rod Langway   D) Serge Savard

12 Winning three major individual NHL awards in a single season is a relatively rare occurrence. Who is the only player in NHL history to win the Art Ross, Hart and Lady Byng Trophies in consecutive seasons?

A) Jean Beliveau   B) Stan Mikita

C) Howie Morenz   D) Wayne Gretzky

1 Who was the youngest goaltender to appear in an NHL match?

A) Harry Lumley   B) Frank Brimsek

C) Rogatien Vachon   D) Terry Sawchuk

2 How many different players have won the Art Ross Trophy as the NHL's leading scorer while a member of the Pittsburgh Penguins?

A) 1   B) 2

C) 3   D) 4

3 Wayne Gretzky of the Edmonton Oilers recorded at least one point in 51 consecutive regular season games during the 1983-1984 season. Who is the only other player in NHL history to record at least a point in over 40 consecutive games?

A) Bobby Orr   B) Guy Lafleur

C) Mario Lemieux   D) Jaromir Jagr

4 In which Winter Olympics did the International Olympic Commitee first permit countries to include professional players on their rosters?

A) 1984   B) 1988

C) 1998   D) 2002

5 Who is sometimes referred to as 'Mario Jr.'?

A) Vincent Lecavalier   B) Sidney Crosby

C) Evgeni Malkin   D) Jaromir Jagr

6 Nicklas Lidstrom of the Detroit Red Wings finished second in voting for the James Norris Memorial Trophy as the NHL's top defenseman three years in a row from 1998 until 2000. Who is the only other player to finish in the runner-up position for the Norris three consecutive times?

A) Mark Howe   B) Brad Park

C) Al MacInnis   D) Brian Leetch

7 Who holds the NHL record for the most career penalty minutes?

A) Dave Schultz   B) Tie Domi
C) Dave Williams   D) Bob Probert

8 Wayne Gretzky, Gordie Howe and Jaromir Jagr all won the Art Ross Trophy as the NHL's leading scorer at least four consecutive times. Who is the only other player to accomplish the feat?

A) Guy Lafleur   B) Stan Mikita
C) Phil Esposito   D) Maurice Richard

9 Who was the last Toronto Maple Leafs goaltender to be named to the NHL's First All-Star Team?

A) Johnny Bower   B) Mike Palmateer
C) Curtis Joseph   D) Felix Potvin

10 Who was the first European-trained goaltender to win the Vezina Trophy as the NHL's top goaltender?

A) Dominik Hasek   B) Pelle Lindbergh
C) Roman Turek   D) Roman Cechmanek

11 Name the Hockey Hall of Fame member who was known as 'The Pembroke Peach'.

A) Newsy Lalonde   B) Aurel Joliet
C) Joe Malone   D) Frank Nighbor

12 How many different NHL teams has Pat Burns coached during his coaching career?

A) 3   B) 4
C) 5   D) 6

1 Who recorded the most career playoff points in the abbreviated history of the World Hockey Association?

A) Gordie Howe   B) Mark Howe

C) Bobby Hull   D) Anders Hedberg

2 Wayne Gretzky led the NHL in assists in a season an amazing 16 times during his career. Who is the only other player to lead the league in assists in a season as many as five times?

A) Mario Lemieux   B) Bobby Orr

C) Stan Mikita   D) Gordie Howe

3 Goaltender, Mike Vernon is one of only two members of the Calgary Flames to have his jersey number retired by the team. Who is the only other Flame to be so honored?

A) Theo Fleury   B) Al MacInnis

C) Lanny McDonald   D) Joe Mullen

4 Who is the only player in NHL history to score on a penalty shot in the Stanley Cup Final?

A) Antoine Vermette   B) Chris Pronger

C) Pavel Bure   D) Joe Sakic

5 Reggie Leach of the Philadelphia Flyers set the NHL record for the most goals scored in a single Stanley Cup Playoff year in 1976 with 19. Who would later tie Leach for this record?

A) Jari Kurri   B) Mike Bossy

C) Joe Sakic   D) Dino Ciccarelli

6 Eddie Shack was one of the NHL's most energetic and agitating players during his playing days. What was Shack's nickname?

A) 'The Clown'   B) 'The Showman'

C) 'The Entertainer'   D) 'The Agitator'

7 On May 10th, 1970 Bobby Orr of the Boston Bruins scored the Stanley Cup winning goal in overtime. The goal is considered to be one of the most famous goals in NHL history. Who assisted on Orr's historic Stanley Cup winning goal?

A) Phil Esposito   B) Ed Westfall
C) Gary Doak   D) Derek Sanderson

8 With which World Hockey Association franchise did Wayne Gretzky begin his professional hockey career?

A) Edmonton Oilers   B) Cincinnati Stingers
C) Indianapolis Racers   D) Houston Aeros

9 In 1974, for the only time in NHL history goaltenders from different teams shared the Vezina Trophy with identical goals against averages. With whom did Bernie Parent of the Philadelphia Flyers share the 1974 Vezina?

A) Ken Dryden   B) Tony Esposito
C) Gilles Gilbert   D) Ed Giacomin

10 Who was the last player in NHL history to score at least 50 goals in a season while playing for two different teams that season?

A) Pierre Larouche   B) Craig Simpson
C) Dave Andreychuk   D) Jaromir Jagr

11 Who set an NHL record when he scored his first NHL goal at the 15 second mark of his first NHL game?

A) Sidney Crosby   B) Mario Lemieux
C) Bill Mosienko   D) Gus Bodnar

12 Denis Potvin of the New York Islanders is one of only two defenseman to be selected first overall in the NHL Entry Draft to go on to capture the Calder Memorial Trophy as the NHL's rookie of the year. Who is the only other player to accomplish this feat?

A) Raymond Bourque   B) Roman Hamrlik
C) Bryan Berard   D) Brian Leetch

1 Who has recorded the most career three or more goal games in the history of the NHL?

A) Maurice Richard   B) Wayne Gretzky

C) Brett Hull   D) Mike Bossy

2 In which season, for the only time in NHL history, did the previous season's Stanley Cup Finalists both fail to qualify for the Stanley Cup Playoffs?

A) 2000-2001   B) 2002-2003

C) 2005-2006   D) 2006-2007

3 Who was the first player in NHL history to receive a salary of at least 15 million dollars for a single season?

A) Joe Sakic   B) Mario Lemieux

C) Jaromir Jagr   D) Eric Lindros

4 How many different players scored at least 50 goals in a single NHL regular season as members of the Pittsburgh Penguins?

A) 3   B) 5

C) 6   D) 7

5 Darryl Sittler of the Toronto Maple Leafs is one of only two players to score six goals in a single regular season NHL game, since 1967. Who is the only other player to accomplish this feat?

A) Bill Goldsworthy   B) Red Berenson

C) Tim Young   D) Yvan Cournoyer

6 Who scored at least one goal in 13 consecutive regular season NHL games during the 1979-80 season, the longest consecutive games-scoring streak in the NHL since the 1920s?

A) Mike Bossy   B) Steve Shutt

C) Rick Middleton   D) Charlie Simmer

7 Who is the only player in history to win the Lady Byng Memorial Trophy as the NHL's most gentlemanly player as both a forward and a defenseman?

A) Frank Boucher   B) Red Kelly
C) Bill Quackenbush   D) Bobby Bauer

8 Which is the only team in NHL history to score a record nine goals in a single period of a regular season game?

A) Minnesota North Stars   B) Buffalo Sabres
C) Philadelphia Flyers   D) Boston Bruins

9 Jean Beliveau is one of only two players to play 20 NHL seasons as a member of the Montreal Canadiens. Who is the only other player to play 20 seasons with the Habs?

A) Yvan Cournoyer   B) Henri Richard
C) Serge Savard   D) Larry Robinson

10 Both Wayne Gretzky and Mario Lemieux scored at least 50 goals in a season, in 50 games or less, three times each during their NHL careers. Who is the only other player in NHL history to score 50 times in 50 games or less, twice in his career?

A) Mike Bossy   B) Teemu Selanne
C) Alexander Mogilny D) Brett Hull

11 Who is the youngest player in history to serve as captain of an NHL team?

A) Brian Bellows   B) Steve Yzerman
C) Vincent Lecavalier D) Sidney Crosby

12 Who was often referred to as 'The China Wall'?

A) Terry Sawchuk   B) Johnny Bower
C) Turk Broda   D) Gump Worsley

1   B – Richard scored 544 goals in 978 games with the Canadiens.

2   A – Selanne scored 47 times for the Anaheim Mighty Ducks to claim the first Richard Trophy.

3   D – Stastny recorded 109 points for the Quebec Nordiques during the 1980-81 season.

4   C – Clark played the final 20 games of his career with the Maple Leafs in 1999-2000.

5   B – LaFontaine recorded 148 points in 1992-93 to set the Sabres record.

6   B – Henri Richard was a member of 11 Stanley Cup Championship teams in his 20 seasons with the Montreal Canadiens.

7   D – Fleury scored the short-handed hat-trick on March 9th, 1991 while a member of the Calgary Flames.

8   C – Salming was named to the NHL First All-Star Team in 1977.

9   B – From 1974-75 until 1979-80, Lafleur scored at least 50 times in a season for the Montreal Canadiens.

10 A – Lecavalier led Canada to the Gold Medal in the 2004 World Cup of Hockey.

11 C – DiPietro was selected first overall by the New York Islanders in the 2000 NHL Entry Draft.

12 C – Probert spent 2090 minutes in the sin-bin while a member of the Red Wings.

1   A – Morenz won the Hart in 1928, 1931 and 1932.

2   C – Coffey played 18 games with the Boston Bruins during the 2000-01 season.

3   B – Orr was just 30 years old when inducted into the Hall of Fame in 1979.

4   B – Howe was 41 years old when he recorded 103 points for the Detroit Red Wings during the 1968-69 season.

5   B – The Red Wings led the NHL in points from the 1948-49 season until the 1954-55 season.

6   D – Larmer played 11 complete seasons with the Hawks without missing a game.

7   A – Leetch won the Calder Trophy in 1989.

8   B – Demers was behind the bench for the Canadiens' Stanley Cup Championship in 1993.

9   B – The Toros played in the WHA from 1973 until 1976.

10   B – Chelios made the NHL First All-Star Team once as a Montreal Canadien, once as a Detroit Red Wing and three times as a member of the Chicago Blackhawks.

11   B – Kerr registered four 50-goal seasons for the Flyers, mostly from the 'Slot'.

12   C – Orr recorded at least 100 points for the Boston Bruins in the regular season from 1969-70 until 1974-75.

1   C – Stevens served as the Devils captain from 1992-93 until 2003-04.

2   C – Green was just 26 years old when he first became coach of the Washington Capitals in 1979.

3   D – Beliveau recorded 176 playoff points in 162 playoff games with the Habs.

4   D – Lacroix recorded 798 points in just 551 games in the WHA.

5   D – Worters won the 1929 Hart Trophy as a member of the New York Americans.

6   A – Bucyk scored 545 times in his 21 seasons with the Bruins.

7   C – Nolan scored two goals in a span of eight seconds during the 1997 NHL All-Star Game.

8   A – Pavelich scored five times for the New York Rangers on February 23rd, 1983.

9   C – Demers won the Adams Award as the coach of the Detroit Red Wings in both 1987 and 1988.

10 D – Lafleur recorded career-point number 1000 in just his 720th NHL game.

11 D – Mogilny won the Lady Byng Trophy in 2003.

12 B – The Bruins chose Dryden with the 14th overall selection of the 1964 Draft.

1   A – Ratelle recorded 109 points for the New York Rangers in 1971-72 and 105 points for the Boston Bruins in 1975-76.

2   B – Lindsay scored three times in the 1950 All-Star Game for the Detroit Red Wings.

3   C – Robert recorded exactly 100 points for the Sabres during the 1974-75 NHL regular season.

4   A – The Canadiens and the Bruins faced each other seven times in the Stanley Cup Final with the Habs winning all seven.

5   D – Lemieux scored 31 power-play goals for the Pittsburgh Penguins in both 1988-89 and 1995-96.

6   C – Nieuwendyk scored five times for the Flames in a game against the Winnipeg Jets on January 11th, 1989.

7   B – Barrasso recorded 48 assists in his 19 seasons in the NHL.

8   A – Richard scored 34 goals for the Montreal Canadiens in just 59 Stanley Cup Final games.

9   B – The Eagles played only the 1934-35 season in the National Hockey League.

10   A – Hull played nine games with the Hartford Whalers in 1979-80 to conclude his magnificent career.

11   C – Stewart retired from the NHL in 1940 with a then record 515 career points.

12   B – In 1970, Orr won the James Norris, Art Ross, Hart and Conn Smythe trophies.

QUIZ 5 Answers

1 D – Trottier of the New York Islanders recorded six points during the second period of a game against the New York Rangers on December 23rd, 1978.

2 D – Recchi recorded 123 points for the Flyers during the 1992-93 regular season.

3 C – Nilan took ten penalties totaling 42 minutes in a game between his Boston Bruins and the Hartford Whalers on March 31st, 1991.

4 B – Tortorella has been the coach of the Lightning since 2001.

5 A – Hull was named to the NHL First All-Star Team ten times during his 16 seasons in the league.

6 D – The Capitals set the NHL record in 1974-75 in just 80 games.

7 C – Gainey played for the Petes from 1971 until 1973, registering just 23 goals in his career with the team.

8 C – Reese of the Calgary Flames registered three assists in a game against the San Jose Sharks on February 10th, 1993.

9 D – Ramsay played all 1070 of his NHL career games with the Sabres.

10 A and B – Both the Kings and the Blackhawks have lost 16 games in a row in the Stanley Cup Playoffs.

11 A – Coffey scored 48 times for the Edmonton Oilers during the 1985-86 season.

12 B – Hull recorded 131 points for the Blues during the 1990-91 season.

1   A – The Capitals, Kevin Hatcher, Al Iafrate and Sylvain Cote all scored more than 20 goals during the 1992-93 season.

2   B – Sutter served as captain of the Blues from 1979 until 1988.

3   A – Peeters went undefeated 27 games in 1979-80 with the Philadelphia Flyers and 31 games with the 1982-83 Boston Bruins.

4   B – The Flames joined the Islanders as expansion teams in 1972-73 to bring the total number of NHL teams to 16.

5   D – Montreal was home to the NHL Draft for the first 22 years.

6   C – Irvin was the coach of the Canadiens from 1940 until 1955.

7   B – Delvecchio played his entire NHL career with Red Wings after joining the team in 1951.

8   A – Kurri was not just a goal scorer as he set up a great deal of Gretzky's goals.

9   D – The Howes played together on the Aeros from 1973 until 1977.

10   C – Horton was a rugged and reliable defenseman for the Leafs for the better part of two decades.

11   B – Douglas won the Calder Trophy in 1963 as a member of the Toronto Maple Leafs.

12   A – Fuhr won 16 playoff games for the Edmonton Oilers in 1988 leading the Oilers to the Stanley Cup.

1   B – Coffey scored 12 times for the Edmonton Oilers during the 1985 Stanley Cup Playoffs.

2   A – A member of the Canadiens has been the leading scorer in the NHL on 16 occasions.

3   C – Bowman won over 1200 games during his NHL coaching career but failed to win 500 games with one team.

4   C – The Vancouver Canucks chose Patrik Sundstrom in the 1980 NHL Entry Draft while the New York Rangers selected his twin brother Peter in the 1981 Entry Draft.

5   D – Lalonde scored six times in a game for the Canadiens on January 20th, 1920.

6   C – Salo recorded a team record 23 shutouts during his tenure with the Oilers.

7   D – Thornton played for the Greyhounds from 1995 until 1997.

8   D – Stastny won the Calder Trophy in 1981 while a member of the Quebec Nordiques.

9   D – Murdoch scored five times for the New York Rangers in a game against the Minnesota North Stars on October 12th, 1976.

10 C – Beliveau made $110,000 a season when he signed with the Montreal Canadiens in 1953.

11 D – The Red Wings won 62 times in 82 games during the 1995-96 NHL regular season.

12 A – Cloutier recorded a hat-trick in his first NHL game in 1979 as a member of the Quebec Nordiques.

1   A – Shero also led the Philadelphia Flyers to the Stanley Cup Championship that season.

2   B – Tikkanen, Gretzky's teammate was known to get under the skin of an opponent with his aggressive play.

3   B – Tocchet spent 1817 minute in the penalty box as a member of the Flyers.

4   A – In 1981-82, Secord scored 44 goals and was assessed 303 minutes in penalties for the Chicago Blackhawks.

5   D – Bossy scored the Stanley Cup winning goal for the New York Islanders in both 1982 and 1983.

6   D – Nieuwendyk scored 31 power-play goals for the Calgary Flames during the 1987-88 season.

7   A – Bower was 44 years old when he recorded the final shutout of his NHL career in 1968-69 with the Toronto Maple Leafs.

8   A – The Bread Line dominated the NHL during the late 1930s.

9   C – Richards was a member of the Rangers from 2001 until 2005.

10   C – LeClair scored at least 50 goals in a season for the Philadelphia Flyers from 1995-96 until 1997-98.

11   D – Lumley recorded 13 shutouts in 1953-54 to establish the Maple Leaf franchise record.

12   B – Johnson was behind the bench for the Bruins when they captured the Stanley Cup in 1972.

QUIZ 9 Answers

1   B – Pilote recorded 59 points for the Chicago Blackhawks in 1964-65.

2   D – Goaltender, Richter backstopped the U.S.A. to the Gold Medal at the 1996 World Cup.

3   D – Stastny recorded 139 points during the 1981-82 regular season for the Nordiques.

4   B – Joliet, though small in stature, was considered to be one of the most feisty players on a superb Montreal Canadiens team during the 1920s and 1930s.

5   C – Cook was the first captain of the Rangers and served as such from 1926 until 1937.

6   C – Reay coached the Chicago Blackhawks for 1012 games from 1963 until 1977.

7   C – The Montreal Canadiens chose Houle first overall in the 1969 NHL Entry Draft and they would capture the Stanley Cup in 1970-71, Houle's rookie year in the NHL.

8   B – Howe won the Hart Trophy in 1952, 1953, 1957, 1958, 1960 and 1963 for a total of six NHL MVP honors.

9   D – The Bruins won the Stanley Cup in 1929, 1939, 1941, 1970 and 1972.

10   D – Getzlaf played for the WHL's Calgary Hitmen from 2001 until 2005.

11   B – The Blazers played in the WHA for only two seasons.

12   C – Beliveau recorded 62 points in 64 Stanley Cup Final games during his career.

1   B – Henri Richard was considered to be a smaller version of his more famous brother, yet would eclipse his brother in Stanley Cup Championships.

2   A – Igilnla eclipsed Al MacInnis' Flames record of 803 games during the 2007-08 season.

3   C – Pronger won both the Hart and Norris trophies in 2000 as a member of the St. Louis Blues.

4   A – Howe scored six times for the Red Wings in a 12-2 victory over the New York Rangers on February 3rd, 1944.

5   B – A member of the Leafs has yet to win the Norris Trophy since it was first awarded in 1954.

6   B – Hall was selected NHL First Team All-Star five times as a member of the Chicago Blackhawks and once each with the Detroit Red Wings and the St. Louis Blues.

7   B – Clarke served as the Panthers general manager in 1993-94.

8   B – A team comprised mainly of Canadians led Great Britain to Olympic Gold in 1936.

9   C – Chelios was named to the NHL's First All-Star Team in 1995-96.

10   C – Harvey served as the Canadiens captain for only one season, 1960-61. He would be traded to the New York Rangers for the following season.

11   A – Ullman scored 42 times for the Red Wings to lead the NHL in 1964-65.

12   A – Philadelphia Flyers' Schultz accumulated over 1000 minutes in penalties in leading the league from 1972-73 until 1974-75.

QUIZ 11 Answers

1 A – Bure scored three penalty-shot goals for the Vancouver Canucks in 1997-98.

2 A – Schmidt spent the better part of 30 years playing for and coaching the Bruins.

3 C – Beliveau was selected to the NHL All-Star Team a total of ten times during his 20-year career.

4 D – Plante won the Vezina Trophy from 1956 until 1960 inclusive.

5 A – Ruff has been the coach of the Sabres since the beginning of the 1997-98 season.

6 D – Forsberg won the Hart Trophy in 2003 in a close race with his countryman Naslund.

7 A – Lemaire coached the Devils from 1993-94 until 1997-98.

8 D – Potvin recorded 101 points for the New York Islanders during the 1978-79 regular season.

9 C – Hull led the NHL in goal scoring seven times in his 15 seasons with the Chicago Blackhawks.

10 C – Howe led the NHL in scoring five times during the 1950s and once during the 1960s.

11 A – Nolan was selected first overall by the Quebec Nordiques in 1990.

12 D – The Leafs opened the Gardens against the Blackhawks in 1931 and played their last game there in 1999 against the Blackhawks.

QUIZ 12 Answers

1   C – Kane played for the OHL's London Knights in 2006-07, leading the league in scoring that season.

2   C – Babych scored 54 times for the Blues during the 1980-81 NHL regular season.

3   B – The Whalers won their only Avco Cup in 1972-73.

4   A – Robitaille scored 125 points for the Los Angeles Kings during the 1992-93 NHL season.

5   B – Dionne scored at least 40 goals in a season ten times during his 18-year NHL career.

6   D – Hainsworth blanked the opponent 75 times during his tenure with the Canadiens.

7   C – Canada won Olympic Gold in 1924, 1928, 1932, 1948, 1952 and 2002.

8   A – Connell registered 15 shutouts for the Ottawa Senators in both 1925-26 and 1927-28.

9   B – The Pirates failed to win the Stanley Cup during their short tenure in the NHL.

10 A – Domi played two games for the Maple Leafs in 1989-90 before being traded to the New York Rangers in 1990.

11 C – Edmonton-born Shore was considered to be the best defenseman in the NHL during his time with the Boston Bruins.

12 C – Langway served as the Capitals captain from 1982 until 1993.

1   D – Selby won the Calder Trophy in 1966.

2   D – Vickers scored three goals and added four assists in a game on February 18th, 1976.

3   C – Fuhr played in the 1982 NHL All-Star Game at the age of 19.

4   D – Bossy scored his 100th NHL goal on February 19th, 1979, in just his 129th game.

5   D – Hull led the NHL in goal scoring from 1989-90 until 1991-92 while a member of the St. Louis Blues.

6   C – Chelios was named to the NHL First All-Star Team in 1995-96.

7   B – Murphy won the Stanley Cup twice with the Pittsburgh Penguins and twice with the Detroit Red Wings during the 1990s.

8   B – Andreychuk scored 270 career goals while his team enjoyed the man advantage.

9   B – Bucyk assisted on 813 goals during his 23 seasons in the NHL.

10   B – The US defeated Finland 4-2 in the final game of 1980 Winter Games to secure the Gold.

11   D – Lemieux recorded 161 points for the Pittsburgh Penguins during the 1995-96 NHL season.

12   A – Hall of the Chicago Blackhawks surrendered Richard's 500th NHL goal on October 19th, 1957.

QUIZ 14 Answers

1   D – Loob scored exactly 50 times for the Calgary Flames during the 1987-88 regular season.

2   B – Muller was taken second overall by the New Jersey Devils.

3   C – Richards scored seven game-winning goals in the 2004 Stanley Cup Playoffs for the Cup winning Tampa Bay Lightning.

4   A – Clapper of the Boston Bruins was inducted into the Hall of Fame in 1947.

5   B – Niedermayer played for the Blazers from 1989 until 1992.

6   A – Naslund recorded 110 points for the Habs during the 1985-86 season.

7   A – Muckler coached the Oilers to the Stanley Cup in 1990.

8   C – Leinonen registered six assists for the New York Rangers in a playoff game on April 8th, 1982.

9   C – Sawchuk began his career with the Detroit Red Wings in 1949 and ended it in 1970 as a member of the New York Rangers.

10   A – Seattle defeated Montreal to claim the 1917 Stanley Cup.

11   D – Belfour did not see any action during the 2002 Winter Games.

12   D – Giguere played eight games for the Whalers during the 1996-97 regular season.

155

1   A – Barber scored 420 goals for the Flyers in his 12 years with the team.

2   D – Taylor played 1111 games for the Kings in 17 seasons with the team.

3   B – The Nationals represented Ottawa in WHA in 1972-73.

4   A – Orr was a majestic skater despite numerous knee injuries that shortened his career.

5   B – Datsyuk was the 171st player selected in the 1998 Draft.

6   B – The Thrashers joined the Southeast Division of the NHL in 1999.

7   D – Robinson recorded a plus 120 with the Montreal Canadiens in 1976-77.

8   D – Vanbiesbrouck was selected to the NHL First All-Star Team in 1986.

9   B – The Red Wings and Maple Leafs have met seven times in the Stanley Cup Final, with the Red Wings emerging victorious just once.

10   A – Day coached the Toronto Maple Leafs to five Stanley Cup Championships during the 1940s

11   D – Hall recorded 12 shutouts for the Red Wings in the 1955-56 NHL regular season.

12   C – Tardif scored 316 goals during his WHA career.

1   C – Muller recorded six points for the Devils in a game on November 29th, 1986.

2   B – Gilmour recorded 127 points for the Maple Leafs during the 1992-93 NHL season.

3   D – Trottier scored five times in a game in both 1978 and 1982.

4   A – Esposito won both the Calder and Vezina in 1970.

5   B – Lafleur won the Award in 1976, 1977 and 1978.

6   C – The Red Wings chose Lidstrom with the 53rd pick of the 1989 Entry Draft.

7   D – Smith lost 48 games for the California Golden Seals in 1970-71.

8   A – Mikita earned 62 assists for the Chicago Blackhawks during the 1966-67 season.

9   C – Bossy scored 309 goals for the Laval National of the QMJHL from 1973 until 1977.

10 C – Perreault scored 512 goals in his 17 seasons as a member of the Sabres.

11 B – The season began with four teams but would be reduced to three following the withdrawal of the Montreal Wanderers after just six games.

12 D – Odelein captained the Blue Jackets from 2000 until 2002.

QUIZ 17 Answers

1   C – Robinson appeared in 227 Stanley Cup Playoff games during his career.

2   A – Francis recorded 1249 assists during his 23-year NHL career.

3   A – Hawerchuk recorded five assists for the Winnipeg Jets in the second period of a game on March 6th, 1984.

4   D – Kerr of the Philadelphia Flyers scored 34 power-play goals during the 1985-86 regular season.

5   D – The NHL has expanded from six teams to 30 teams in the past 40 some years.

6   B – Bruins began play in the NHL in 1924-25 season.

7   A – Hunter was penalized 729 minutes in his 186 career playoff games.

8   B – Coffey recorded 196 points in 194 playoff games during his NHL career.

9   D – Gaborik was chosen 3rd overall by the Wild in the 2000 NHL Entry Draft.

10 D – Smith of the New York Islanders was renowned for chopping at the legs of opponents who dared to venture near his crease.

11 A – Thomas scored a total of 13 regular season overtime goals during his NHL career.

12 B – Coffey recorded 37 points for the Edmonton Oilers during the 1985 Stanley Cup Playoffs.

1   C – The NHL now limits the number of players inducted to four.

2   D – Tretiak was superb as the Soviet Union defeated Canada 8-1 in the one-game final.

3   B – Richard recorded five goals and three assists for the Montreal Canadiens in a game against the Detroit Red Wings on December 28th, 1944.

4   B – The Blackhawks won the Stanley Cup in 1934, 1938 and 1961.

5   C – Sheppard scored 52 times for the Red Wings in 1993-94.

6   B – Crosby was four months short of his 19th birthday when he recorded 102 points for the Pittsburgh Penguins in 2005-06.

7   D – Fontinato spent 202 minutes in the penalty box during the 1955-56 regular season.

8   B – Arbour won 739 games in his 19 seasons as the coach of the New York Islanders.

9   C – The Flames acquired Iginla from the Dallas Stars in exchange for Joe Nieuwendyk.

10   B – Savard won the Conn Smythe in 1969 as a member of the Montreal Canadiens.

11   A – Howell played 1160 regular season games with the Rangers.

12   B – Helmets became mandatory for new players in the NHL in 1979.

1   C – The Maple Leafs have won six of the seven Stanley Cup Finals against the Red Wings.

2   B – Kovalchuk was selected first overall by the Atlanta Thrashers in 2001.

3   A – Tessier won the Adams Award in 1983.

4   B – Cournoyer scored 428 goals as a member of the Canadiens.

5   C – The Nordiques left for Colorado in 1995.

6   C – Ullman scored two goals five seconds apart for the Detroit Red Wings on April 11th, 1965, against the Chicago Blackhawks.

7   D – The Islanders went to the Stanley Cup Finals from 1980 until 1984 inclusive.

8   D – Esposito led the NHL in goal scoring from the 1969-70 season until the 1974-75 season.

9   A – LeClair was traded to the Philadelphia Flyers from the Montreal Canadiens during the 1994-95 season.

10   B – The Flames beat the Canadiens in six games in 1989.

11   A – Liut won the Pearson Award in 1981 as a member of the St. Louis Blues.

12   B – Steve Yzerman, Brendan Shanahan and Nicklas Lidstrom were named to the NHL First All-Star Team in 1999-2000.

QUIZ 20 Answers

1 C – Lacroix played 551 games in the WHA during his career.

2 C – Horner received his 1000th career penalty minute in 1936-37.

3 A – Ratelle tallied 109 points for the Rangers during the 1971-72 regular season.

4 D – Langway earned the nickname while manning the blue line for the Washington Capitals during the 1980s.

5 B – Ovechkin was not eligible for the 2003 Draft as he was not old enough.

6 C – Sittler played 61 games for the Detroit Red Wings in 1984-85.

7 D – Parent won both the 1974 and 1975 Conn Smythe trophies as a member of the Philadelphia Flyers.

8 A – Thornton recorded 96 assists in 2005-06 and 92 helpers in 2006-07.

9 A – The Canadiens lost just eight times in 80 games during the 1976-77 season.

10 C – Crosby recorded 102 points and was penalized 110 minutes in 2005-06.

11 C – Chelios won the Norris Trophy in 1989 as a member of the Habs.

12 B – Gretzky won the Trophy on the strength of his 110-point rookie season.

1 B – Bossy played for the National from 1973 until 1977.

2 A – Sjoberg captained the 1979-80 Winnipeg Jets.

3 C – Howe wore 17 when he first entered the NHL in 1946.

4 B – Crozier won the Conn Smythe Trophy in 1966 as a member of the Detroit Red Wings.

5 A – Olmstead recorded eight points in a game against the Chicago Blackhawks on January 9th, 1954.

6 A – Ovechkin was named to the NHL First All-Star Team in both 2006 and 2007.

7 D – Sundin recorded at least one point in 30 consecutive games while a member of the Quebec Nordiques in 1992-93.

8 A – Gilmour played one game for the Maple Leafs in 2003 before an injury ended his NHL career.

9 D – Schultz was a punishing fighter during his days as a Philadelphia Flyer, thus the nickname 'The Hammer'.

10 D – Lemieux scored 13 times while his Penguins were short a man during the 1988-89 season.

11 D – Howe was the captain of the Red Wings from 1958 until 1962.

12 D – Kurri recorded four hat-tricks in the 1985 Stanley Cup Playoffs for the Edmonton Oilers.

QUIZ 22 Answers

1. B – Datsyuk of the Detroit Red Wings won the Lady Byng Trophy in both 2006 and 2007.

2. C – Mikita scored 541 times for the Blackhawks in his 22 seasons with the team.

3. C – Koivu became the captain of the Habs in 1999.

4. A – Fuhr had 14 assists for the Edmonton Oilers during the 1983-84 season.

5. A – Smith recorded 114 points for the Stars during the 1981-82 season.

6. B – Sundin led the Sweden team to the Gold Medal in 2006.

7. C – The Senators lost 38 straight regular season games on the road in 1992-93.

8. A – The Canadiens selected Price 5th overall in the 2005 Entry Draft.

9. B – Esposito recorded 15 shutouts for the Chicago Blackhawks in 1969-70.

10. C – The 2005 Entry Draft was known as 'The Sidney Crosby Sweepstakes'.

11. B – Naslund of the Montreal Canadiens recorded five assists in the 1988 NHL All-Star Game.

12. D – Malkin of the Pittsburgh Penguins scored at least once in the first six games of the 2006-07 season.

1   C – Bourque recorded 17 points in 19 All-Star Game appearances.

2   A – Johson was selected first overall by the St. Louis Blues in 2006 NHL Entry Draft.

3   A – Juneau recorded 102 points for the Boston Bruins in 1992-93.

4   A – Thornton was traded from the Boston Bruins to the San Jose Sharks in 2005-06, winning the Art Ross Trophy that season.

5   D – Boucher went 332 minutes without allowing a goal as a member of the Phoenix Coyotes during the 2003-04 season.

6   D – Zetterberg was chosen 210th overall in the 1999 NHL Entry Draft.

7   B – The US defeated Canada in the Finals of the 1996 World Cup of Hockey.

8   D – Smith was the captain of the Oilers from 2001 until 2007.

9   C – Horton's number 2 was retired by the Sabres following his death in a tragic automobile accident in 1974.

10   C – Beliveau won the Stanley Cup ten times as a player with the Montreal Canadiens and seven times as an executive with the Canadiens.

11   A – The Maple Leafs have had seven forwards, one defenseman and one goaltender win rookie of the year honors in the NHL.

12   B – Gilmour won the Selke Trophy in 1993.

QUIZ 24 Answers

1   D – Hull scored 610 times in the NHL and 303 times in the WHA.

2   A – Fetisov is considered the best Russian defenseman of all time.

3   A – Ovechkin set the record in 2005-06 as a member of the Washington Capitals

4   D – Hollett scored exactly 20 goals for the Detroit Red Wings during the 1944-45 regular season.

5   C – Yzerman recorded 1063 assists in his 23 seasons with the Red Wings.

6   C – Brodeur has won at least 40 games in a season six times as of the end of the 2006-07 regular season.

7   C – Richard became the first hockey player to win the Lou Marsh Trophy when he won it in 1957.

8   C – The Rangers retired Leetch's number 2 on January 24, 2008.

9   C – Smith won the Vezina Trophy in 1982.

10 C – Cournoyer scored five goals in a game against the Chicago Blackhawks on February 15th, 1975.

11 A – The Winter Hawks won the 1983 Memorial Cup.

12 B – The Islanders streak lasted from 1980 until 1984 when they were defeated by the Edmonton Oilers in the Stanley Cup Final.

1   B – Paul Stastny of the Colorado Avalanche set the record in 2006-07.

2   D – Tretiak was inducted into the Hockey Hall of Fame in 1989.

3   B – Imlach spent 12 seasons behind the bench of the Maple Leafs.

4   A – Nicholls scored 70 times for the Kings in 1988-89.

5   D – Henry won the Calder Trophy in 1954 as a member of the New York Rangers.

6   B – Chelios has took part in the Stanley Cup Playoffs in 23 different years up to and including 2008.

7   B – Nilan was one of the NHL's top pugilists during the 1980s and early 1990s.

8   C – Crosby won CHL Player of the Year honors in both 2003-04 and 2004-05.

9   C – Richard finished runner-up in NHL scoring five times during the 1940s and 1950s.

10   B – Keon won the Lady Byng Trophy twice and the Deveau Trophy once during his career.

11   B – The Calder Cup has been awarded to the playoff Champions of the AHL since 1937.

12   C – Bobby Orr with eight and Raymond Bourque with five combined to win 13 Norris trophies with the Bruins.

1   A – Brimsek recorded 80 shutouts in just ten seasons in the NHL.

2   D – Gretzky won the Marsh Trophy a total of four times.

3   C – Jagr won the Art Ross from 1997-98 until 2000-01 inclusive.

4   C – Turnbull scored five times in a game against the Detroit Red Wings on February 2nd, 1977.

5   D – Yzerman played for the Petes from 1981 until 1983.

6   B – Brodeur scored his game-winning goal on February 15th, 2000.

7   C – Bowman began his NHL coaching career with the St. Louis Blues in 1967 and ended it with the Detroit Red Wings in 2000.

8   A – Lindsay won the art Ross Trophy in 1950 with 78 points.

9   B – Lemieux scored four times in the third period of a game against the Montreal Canadiens on January 26th, 1997.

10   D – Murphy went to Michigan State University and was selected first overall in the 1986 Entry Draft by the Detroit Red Wings.

11   A – Frank won MVP honors in 1963 and 1969 while his brother Peter won the award in 1976.

12   D – Hull scored his 500th NHL goal in just his 693rd game.

1 B – Souray scored 19 times while his Montreal Canadiens enjoyed a man advantage during the 2006-07 regular season.

2 A – Beliveau was runner-up for the Hart Trophy in 1957, 1966, 1968 and 1969.

3 C – Sittler recorded 18 three or more goal games in his 12 seasons with the Maple Leafs.

4 D – The Jets won the WHA title in 1976, 1978 and 1979.

5 B – Fedorov recorded NHL point 1000 on February 14th, 2004, in his 965th NHL game.

6 A – The Canadiens won at least 50 games a season from 1975-76 until 1978-1979.

7 C – The Rangers selected Lundqvist 205th in the 2000 Entry Draft.

8 A – Durnan of the Montreal Canadiens was a First Team NHL All-Star from 1943-44 until 1946-47.

9 D – The Petes have had the most players selected in the Entry Draft as of 2007.

10 D – The Rangers won the Stanley Cup in 1940 and did not win it again until 1994.

11 B – Bossy recorded 35 points for the New York Islanders in the 1981 Stanley Cup Playoffs.

12 A – Ciccarelli recorded two playoff hat-tricks for each of the Minnesota North Stars, Washington Capitals and the Detroit Red Wings.

1   A – The NHL schedule was reduced to 48 games in 1994.

2   B – Hainsworth shut out the opponent 22 times in just 44 games for the Montreal Canadiens in the 1928-29 season.

3   D – Howe appeared in the Stanley Cup Playoffs 19 times with the Detroit Red Wings and once with the Hartford Whalers.

4   D – Shore won NHL MVP honors in 1933, 1935, 1936 and 1938.

5   B – Perreault won the Lady Byng Trophy in 1973.

6   C – Neely score 50 goals in just 49 games for the Bruins in 1993-94.

7   B – Lindstrom of the Winnipeg Jets scored five times in a game against the Philadelphia Flyers on March 2nd, 1982.

8   D – Blake coached the Canadiens to five consecutive Stanley Cups from 1956 until 1960.

9   B – Lemieux led the Canadians to the Gold Medal in 2002.

10   A – Unger played in 914 consecutive NHL games from 1968 until 1979.

11   D – Bourque was the captain of the Bruins from 1988 until 2000.

12   D – Beliveau recorded NHL career point number 1000 on March 3rd, 1968.

1   B – The game started on the eve of Easter and ended on Easter.

2   A – Carson scored 55 goals for the Los Angeles Kings in 1987-88 while still in his teens.

3   D – Bure was chosen 113th overall in the 1989 Entry Draft by the Canucks.

4   A – Leach of the Philadelphia Flyers scored 15 goals in his ten-game streak during the 1976 Stanley Cup Playoffs.

5   B – The Bruins have yet to retire the jersey number of a goaltender.

6   C – Nieuwendyk scored five times in a game against the Winnipeg Jets on January 11th, 1989.

7   B – The Avalanche set the record in 2006-07.

8   C – Ciccarelli scored 14 times in 19 games for the Minnesota North Stars during the 1981 Stanley Cup Playoffs.

9   A – The Islanders chose Luongo with the 4th overall pick of the 1997 Entry Draft from QMJHL's Foreurs

10 D – Drillon led the NHL in scoring in 1938.

11 A – Chelios topped the 1500 game mark in 2006-07.

12 B – Weight recorded 104 points for the Oilers in 1995-96.

1   C – A member of the Rangers has won the Lady Byng Trophy 14 times.

2   D – Lemieux scored just 43 times in 1984-85, his rookie year in the NHL.

3   D – Lumley shut out the opponent 13 times during the 1953-54 regular season.

4   C – The Devils won the Stanley Cup in 1995, 2000 and 2003.

5   D – Pilote served as the captain of the Blackhawks from 1961 until 1968.

6   A – Guerin won All-Star MVP honors in 2001.

7   D – Kurri recorded 233 points in the Stanley Cup Playoffs during his career.

8   A – Tonelli led Canada to the 1984 Canada Cup Gold Medal.

9   D – The Maple Leafs chose Kaberle 204th overall in the 1996 NHL Entry Draft.

10   B – Jarvis played 964 consecutive NHL games, never missing a game in his entire NHL career.

11   A – Mahovlich recorded a team record 82 assists during the 1974-75 regular season.

12   C – Lecavalier played for the Oceanic from 1996 until 1998 while Richards played for the team from 1997 until 2000.

1   B – Staal scored seven short-handed goals for the Pittsburgh Penguins in 2006-07.

2   D – Bossy scored at least 50 times in a season for the New York Islanders from 1977-78 until 1985-86.

3   C – Berenson scored six goals in a game against the Philadelphia Flyers on November 7th, 1968.

4   B – Horner led the NHL in penalty minutes from the 1932-33 season until the 1939-40 season.

5   C – Gretzky recorded at least 200 points in a season four times during the 1980s while a member of the Edmonton Oilers.

6   C – Carlyle won the Norris Trophy in 1981.

7   C – Dionne scored ten short-handed goals for the Red Wings in 1974-75.

8   A – Beck scored 22 goals in 1977-78 for the Colorado Rockies.

9   D – Dryden won the Calder Trophy in 1972.

10   C – Morenz's career with the Canadiens was over before the formation of the 'Punch Line'.

11   B – Orr recorded at least 100 points in a season from 1969-70 until 1974-75.

12   D – Parent won 47 games for the Philadelphia Flyers in 1973-74.

1   A – Belfour shut out the opposition 10 times during the 2003-04 regular season.

2   A – Shanahan was the Devils 1st choice, 2nd overall in the 1987 NHL Entry Draft.

3   C – Neilson coached in exactly 1000 games with eight different teams during his NHL coaching career.

4   B – Bure possessed outstanding speed and incredible hands, scoring 437 goals in his 12 seasons in the NHL.

5   C – The 1951 Stanley Cup Final saw the Maple Leafs defeat the Canadiens four games to one with each game needing overtime to be decided.

6   B – The Oilers scored a record 36 goals while short-handed during the 1983-84 season.

7   C – Gamble of the Toronto Maple Leafs won All-Star Game MVP honors in 1968.

8   A – Beliveau signed with the Canadiens as a free agent on October 3rd, 1953.

9   A – Kasper won the Selke Trophy in 1982.

10   D – Coffey played for nine different teams during his 21 year NHL career.

11   B – Brind'amour won the Selke Trophy in both 2006 and 2007 as a member of the Carolina Hurricanes.

12   C – Messier played five games for the Racers in 1978-79 before joining the Cincinnati Stingers after the Racers folded.

1 D – Hitchcock won the Stanley Cup with the Stars in his fourth season with the team.

2 C – The Quebec Nordiques chose Sundin first overall in the 1989 NHL Entry Draft.

3 B – Vanbiesbrouck won 374 regular season games during his NHL career.

4 B – Cherry played in a Stanley Cup Playoff game for the Bruins in 1954-55.

5 B – Beliveau was the first NHL player to appear on the cover of Sports Illustrated.

6 C – Hall played in 502 consecutive complete games for the Detroit Red Wings and the Chicago Blackhawks from 1955 until 1962.

7 D – Salming registered 620 assists in his 16 seasons with the Maple Leafs.

8 C – Robitaille joined the Kings in 1986 long after the 'Triple Crown Line' was dismantled.

9 A – 14 Players scored at least 50 goals in 1992-93 led by Teemu Selanne and Alexander Mogilny with 76 apiece.

10 C – Keon scored twice while his Maple Leafs were down a man in a game against the Detroit Red Wings on April 18th, 1963.

11 B – Arbour coached the St. Louis Blues in three seasons and the New York Islanders for 19 seasons.

12 B – Arnott scored the Stanley Cup winning goal for the New Jersey Devils in 2000.

1   C – Lumley had rosy cheeks especially when in the heat of a game.

2   B – Potvin was the captain of the Islanders from 1979 until 1987.

3   C – Francis scored over 500 career points for both the Hartford Whaler/Carolina Hurricanes and the Pittsburgh Penguins during his career.

4   B – Pronovost recorded 104 points for the Penguins in 1975-76.

5   D – Trottier went 18 straight recording at least a point during the 1981 Stanley Cup Playoffs.

6   C – The Soviet Union won the World Junior Championships from 1974 until 1980 inclusive.

7   A – The 1977-78 Bruins saw 11 members score at least 20 goals.

8   D – Adams won the Stanley Cup as a player in 1918 and 1927 and won three Stanley Cup's as coach and general manager of the Detroit Red Wings during the 1930s and 1940s.

9   A – Malone scored at least five goals in a game twice in 1917-18 and twice in 1919-20.

10 D – Niedermayer won the Norris Trophy as a Devil in 2004.

11 A – Bure recorded 110 points for the Canucks in 1992-93.

12 B – The Sabres and Canucks both failed to make the Stanley Cup Playoffs in their inaugural season in the NHL.

1   A – The Blazers won the Memorial Cup in both 1994 and 1995.

2   D – Richer scored 51 times for the Habs in 1989-90.

3   A – Verbeek got under the skin of many opponents while scoring 522 goals during his NHL career.

4   A – Crozier won the Calder Trophy in 1965.

5   B – Hasek blanked 11 different teams while a member of 1997-98 Buffalo Sabres.

6   A – The Maple Leafs won the Stanley Cup in 1947, 1948 and 1949.

7   D – Parent's number 1 was retired by the Philadelphia Flyers.

8   B – The Cowboys represented the city of Calgary in the WHA.

9   C – Oates recorded a total of 1420 points in his 19 NHL seasons.

10 A – Sheppard score at least 20 goals in a season for Buffalo, New York Rangers, Detroit, San Jose, Florida and Carolina.

11 D – Nilsson recorded a club record 131 points for the Calgary Flames in 1980-81.

12 D – Burns won the Adams Award in 1989 with Montreal, 1993 with Toronto and 1998 with Boston.

QUIZ 36 Answers

1   A – Incredibly the Kings selected Glavine ahead of future superstar Luc Robitaille.

2   D – Howe played in 23 NHL All-Star Games, 22 as a member of the Detroit Red Wings and one as a member of the Hartford Whalers.

3   C – Keon would serve as Maple Leaf captain until 1974-75.

4   B – Wayne Gretzky won the Conn Smythe Trophy twice while Mark Messier and Bill Ranford won it once each.

5   A – Guidolin was just 16 years old when he first suited up for the 1942-43 Boston Bruins.

6   D – Although named to the 1972 Team Canada, Dionne did not participate in any of the eight game Series.

7   B – Roenick recorded just 596 points in his eight seasons with the Blackhawks.

8   B – Five members of the Canadiens have combined to win a total of 11 Norris trophies.

9   D – Roy was the victim of all three milestone goals.

10 A – The 1984-85 Edmonton Oilers saw Wayne Gretzky score 73 times and Jari Kurri add 71 goals.

11 C – Masterton died on January 15th, 1968, following a head injury he suffered in a game against the California Golden Seals two days previously.

12 C – The two-referee system was used on a part-time basis in 1999-2000.

1 C – Barber scored 420 goals in just 12 seasons with the Flyers.

2 A – Bettman became the first Commissioner of the NHL in February 1993.

3 D – The Courtnall's would later be joined as the only brothers to play in 1000 NHL games each by Ron and Brent Sutter.

4 C – Mosienko scored three times in just 21 seconds for the Chicago Blackhawks in a game against New York Rangers on March 23rd, 1952.

5 A – Sakic recorded 102 points in 1989-90 for the Quebec Nordiques who finished in the basement of the NHL with just 31 points.

6 D – Pronger played for the OHL's Petes from 1991 until 1993.

7 B – Roy Conacher, Bobby Hull and Stan Mikita are only Blackhawks to win the Art Ross Trophy since it was first awarded in 1948.

8 A – Fedorov scored all five Detroit Red Wings goals in a game against the Washington Capitals on December 26th, 1996.

9 D – Sundstrom scored one goal and added six assists in a game on February 29th, 1984.

10 B – Bowman won 223 Stanley Cup Playoff games during his career.

11 A – Both Lindros and Jagr recorded 70 points with Jagr outscoring Lindros 32 to 29.

12 D – Harrison recorded a record ten points in a game for the Edmonton Oilers to set the WHA record.

1   A – Nicklas Lidstrom and Chris Chelios of the Red Wings were named to the NHL First All-Star Team in 2001-02.

2   B – Esposito potted goal number 600 early in the 1977-78 season while a member of the New York Rangers.

3   A – Jagr recorded 149 points for the Pittsburgh Penguins in 1995-96.

4   D – Kelly won the Stanley Cup four times with the Detroit Red Wings in the 1950s and four times with the Toronto Maple Leafs in the 1960s.

5   A – Hawerchuk scored his 500th NHL goal on January 31st, 1996 as a member of the Blues.

6   D – Taylor of the Detroit Red Wings recorded seven assists in a game against the Chicago Blackhawks on March 16th, 1947.

7   B – Howe won the Art Ross Trophy from 1951 until 1954 inclusive.

8   C – Alfredsson won the Calder Trophy in 1996.

9   B – Brimsek won both trophies in 1939 as a member of the Boston Bruins.

10 B – Roenick recorded 107 points for the Blackhawks in 1993-94.

11 A – Bobby Orr and Raymond Bourque combined to win 13 Norris trophies as Boston Bruins.

12 B – Iginla played for the Blazers from 1993 until 1996.

1   C – Bowman coached in the NHL All-Star Game 13 times during his career.

2   A – Conacher was a prolific goal scorer for the Toronto Maple leafs during the 1930s.

3   D – Domi set the Maple Leaf record in just ten full seasons with the team.

4   A – Beliveau of the Montreal Canadiens won the 1965 Conn Smythe Trophy.

5   D – Pagnutti was 20.6 years of age when selected by the Los Angeles Kings in 1967.

6   D – Salming played 49 games for the Detroit Red Wings in 1989-90.

7   D – Staal was just 18.6 years of age when he recorded his first NHL hat-trick during the 2006-07 season.

8   C – Numminen has appeared in over 1250 games during his NHL career.

9   B – Brown played the last NHL game without a mask on April 7th, 1974.

10   B – Carpenter scored 53 goals for the Washington Capitals during the 1984-85 season.

11   C – Jackman won the Calder Trophy in 2003.

12   D – Coffey recorded NHL point number 1000 as a Penguin on December 22nd, 1990.

1   B – Oates recorded his 1000th NHL point on October 8th, 1997 as a member of the Caps.

2   D – Turnbull scored five times for the Toronto Maple Leafs in a game against Detroit Red Wings on February 2nd, 1977.

3   C – The Forum hosted its first NHL game on November 29th, 1924.

4   A – Sawchuk would go on to win a total of 447 games during his NHL career.

5   D – Kovalchuk was chosen first overall by the Atlanta Thrashers in 2001.

6   A – Patrick led the NHL in goal scoring in 1941-42.

7   D – Richard scored 34 goals for the Montreal Canadiens in 59 Stanley Cup Final games.

8   B – Roy was just 20 years old when he won the Conn Smythe Trophy with the Montreal Canadiens in 1986.

9   B – Brooks was behind the bench for the United States 'Miracle on Ice' in 1980.

10   D – Sittler recorded exactly 100 points for the Maple leafs in 1975-76.

11   C – Lidstrom took over as captain of the Red Wings in 2006-07.

12   A – Trottier of the New York Islanders won the Art Ross Trophy in 1978-79 with 134 points.

QUIZ 41 Answers

1   A – Lemieux played for Voisins from 1981 until 1984 recording an amazing 562 points in the three seasons.

2   B – Nieuwendyk won the Conn Smythe Trophy in 1999.

3   C – Gilmour played for seven different NHL teams during his 20 year career.

4   A – The Blackhawks would finish atop the Western Conference in 1970-71.

5   C – Richard scored his 500th NHL goal against Glenn Hall of the Chicago Blackhawks on October 19th, 1957.

6   C – The Flyers took Forsberg with the sixth overall pick of the 1991 Draft.

7   A – Grant won the Calder Trophy in 1969 as a member of the Minnesota North Stars after being a member of 1968 Stanley Cup Champion Montreal Canadiens.

8   B – Quinn won the Adams Award in 1980 with the Philadelphia Flyers and the 1992 Adams Award with the Vancouver Canucks.

9   C – The 1987 Entry Draft was held at the Joe Louis Arena in Detroit, Michigan.

10   D – Simmer tied Danny Gare and Blaine Stoughton for the NHL lead in goal scoring in 1979-80.

11   A – Both teams were quite futile during the era missing the Stanley Cup Playoffs with great regularity.

12   C – Sawchuk was of Ukrainian descent, thus the nickname.

1   A – Crosby played for the Oceanic from 2003 until 2005.

2   D – Salming was named to the NHL First All-Star Team in 1976-77.

3   B – Blake recorded 47 points in 48 games for the Montreal Canadiens to lead the NHL in scoring in 1938-39.

4   C – Kerr's tenure with the Flyers preceded the formation of the Flyers' 'Legion of Doom'.

5   C – Cherry coached the Rockies one season, 1979-80.

6   A – Orr won the Hart Trophy in 1970, 1971 and 1972.

7   D – Gretzky won the Hart Trophy eight consecutive times from 1980 thru 1987.

8   A – In 1960-61, Jean Beliveau was named to the NHL First All-Star Team and fellow Hab centerman Henri Richard was named to the Second Team.

9   D – Jarome Iginla joined six other Flames as 50-goal scorers in 2002.

10   D – Ed Johnston of the Boston Bruins played every minute of the 70-game schedule in 1963-64.

11   A – Fedorov recorded his 1000th NHL point on February 14th, 2004.

12   B – The Senators became the St. Louis Eagles in 1934.

1   B – McCabe spent one and a half seasons with the Canucks.

2   B – Leetch recorded 102 points for the New York Rangers in 1991-92.

3   C – Bowman made coaching stops in St. Louis, Montreal, Buffalo, Pittsburgh and Detroit during his career.

4   D – Richard scored all five Montreal Canadiens goals in a playoff game against the Toronto Maple Leafs on March 23rd, 1944.

5   B – Hainsworth was the captain of the Canadiens for the 1932-33 season.

6   C – The Soviet Union won the Challenge Cup played at Madison Square Garden in New York City.

7   C – Goaltender Broda played a total of 101 Stanley Cup Playoff games for the Toronto Maple Leafs.

8   B – Howe recorded 95 points for the Detroit Red Wings in 1952-53.

9   C – Rick Vaive, Gary Leeman and Dave Andreychuk are the only Maple Leafs to score at least 50 goals in a season.

10   D – Peluso was penalized 408 minutes for the Chicago Blackhawks in 1991-92.

11   C – Phaneuf played with Rebels of the WHL from 2001 until 2005.

12   D – Damphousse won NHL All-Star MVP honors in 1991.

1 B – Lemieux scored his 500th NHL goal on a penalty shot against Tommy Soderstrom of the New York Islanders on October 26th, 1995.

2 B – Beliveau has been the face of the Montreal Canadiens for the better part of six decades.

3 D – Gretzky won the Lady Byng Trophy once in Edmonton, three times in Los Angeles and once for the New York Rangers.

4 A – The Flames won the Stanley Cup in 1989 after relocating from Atlanta in 1980.

5 A – Bourque scored 410 goals during his 22-year NHL career.

6 B – Hall was named to NHL First All-Star Team seven times and the Second Team four times.

7 B – Bossy scored at least 60 goals in a regular season five times in his ten years in the NHL.

8 C – Langway joined the Canadiens after 'The Big Three' led the Canadiens to four consecutive Stanley Cup Championships in the 1970s.

9 C – Mario Lemieux, Jaromir Jagr and Sidney Crosby are the only Penguins to win the Hart Trophy as of the 2006-07 season.

10 D – Henderson also scored the game and series winner in game eight of the historic series.

11 B – Harvey played 70 games for the Blues in 1968-69.

12 A – Bure won the Richard Trophy in both 2000 and 2001.

QUIZ 45 Answers

1   D – Keon won the 1967 Conn Smythe Trophy leading the Maple Leafs to their last Championship.

2   B – The Rangers won the Stanley Cup in 1928, 1933, 1940 and 1994.

3   A – Perreault was chosen by the Buffalo Sabres first overall in the Entry Draft in 1970 and won the Calder Trophy in 1970-71.

4   B – Esposito set the record in 1970-71 as a member of the Boston Bruins.

5   C – Lemieux scored five times for the Pittsburgh Penguins in a game against the Philadelphia Flyers on April 25th, 1989.

6   A – Richard won the Hart Trophy in 1947.

7   B – Hall was 36 years old when he won the Conn Smythe Trophy in 1968 as a member of the St. Louis Blues.

8   C – Mortson and Thomson helped the Toronto Maple Leafs to four Stanley Cup Championships.

9   A – The Sedin twins were selected by the Vancouver Canucks second and third overall in the 1999 Entry Draft.

10   D – The Sharks lost 71 of the 84 games they played during the 1992-93 regular season.

11   C – Staal played for the Petes from 2001 until 2003.

12   A – Geoffrion of the Montreal Canadiens scored 50 times in 1960-61.

1　C – The Red Wings chose Datsyuk 171st overall in the 1998 Entry Draft.

2　D – Ted Lindsay, Sid Abel and Gordie Howe finished the 1949-50 season as top three point producers in the NHL.

3　D – Salming was inducted into the Hockey Hall of Fame in 1996.

4　A – Bailey suffered a career-ending head injury in a game against the Boston Bruins on December 12th, 1933.

5　C – Alexander Ovechkin joined four other Capitals as a member of the 50-goal club in 2005-06.

6　C – Gorman won the Stanley Cup with the Chicago Blackhawks in 1934 and the Montreal Maroons in 1935.

7　B – Sakic won both trophies in 2001 as a member of the Colorado Avalanche.

8　D – The Mariners played in the WHA for three seasons before folding.

9　B – Madden won the Selke Trophy in 2001.

10　C – The NHL season was reduced to 82 games from 84 in 1995-96.

11　C – Coffey scored nine short-handed goals for the Edmonton Oilers in 1985-86.

12　D – Harvey won the Norris Trophy six times with the Montreal Canadiens and once with the New York Rangers.

1   B – The United States won Olympic Gold in both 1960 and 1980.

2   B – Dryden won the Calder Trophy in 1972.

3   D – The Wild accomplished the feat in 2003, coming back in both the first and second rounds of the Stanley Cup Playoffs that season.

4   D – Mikita won the Art Ross Trophy in 1964, 1965, 1967 and 1968.

5   A – Dryden won six Stanley Cup rings as a member of the Montreal Canadiens in the 1970s.

6   D – Nilsson recorded 131 points for the Flames in 1980-81.

7   A – The Maple Leafs are the only 'Original Six' team to fail to have a player win the Norris Trophy.

8   D – Bucyk was just short of 36 years old when he scored 51 goals for the Boston Bruins in 1970-71.

9   D – Raycroft won the Calder Trophy in 2004 as a member of the Boston Bruins.

10 C – Sundin scored five goals and added four assists for Sweden to lead all scorers at the 2002 Olympic games.

11 D – Hall is considered to be one of the greatest goaltenders in NHL history.

12 B – Esposito recorded his 100th point of the 1968-69 season on March 2nd, 1969, on his way to a (then) record 126 points.

1   B – Schultz spent 472 minutes in the sin-bin for the Philadelphia Flyers during the 1974-75 season.

2   C – Lindros played for the Oshawa Generals from 1989 until 1992.

3   B – The Stanley Cup came under the control of the NHL to begin the 1926-27 season.

4   B – Ullman led the NHL in goal scoring with 42 in 1964-65.

5   A – Meeker scored five times for the Toronto Maple Leafs in a game against the Chicago Blackhawks on January 8th, 1947.

6   A – Martin scored 52 goals for the Sabres in 1973-74.

7   C – Lawton was selected first overall in the 1983 NHL Entry Draft by the Minnesota North Stars.

8   A – Wilson was the captain of the Sharks from 1991 until 1993.

9   A – Tkachuk scored 52 goals for the Phoenix Coyotes during the 1996-97 regular season.

10 B – The 1987-1988 Flames saw Joe Nieuwendyk, Hakan Loob, Mike Bullard and Joe Mullen score at least 40 times during the season.

11 A – Esposito was 26 years old when he won the Calder Trophy as a Member of the Chicago Blackhawks in 1970.

12 B – Pulford was named the first president of the NHLPA in 1967.

1 D – Clarke of the Philadelphia Flyers won the first of his three Hart trophies in 1973.

2 D – Fuhr played 23 games for the Calgary Flames in 1999-2000.

3 C – Hunter recorded 1020 points and 3565 penalty minutes in his 19-year NHL career.

4 B – Forsberg totaled 42 points for Sweden during his World Junior career.

5 D – Cashman ended his NHL career as a member of the Boston Bruins in 1983.

6 B – Morenz was a dominant player in the NHL during the 1920s and 1930s before suffering a career-ending leg injury in 1937.

7 C – Howe won the Art Ross Trophy in 1963 with a total of 86 points.

8 C – Bossy led the NHL in goal scoring in 1978-79 with 69 and 1980-81 with 68.

9 A – Anderson was an integral cog on the Oilers when they won their five Stanley Cup titles .

10 B – Chelios' stellar NHL career led to him being named captain of the last three US Olympic Teams.

11 B – Kennedy won the Hart Trophy in 1955.

12 C – MacTavish played without a helmet his entire career, ending his NHL career with the St. Louis Blues in 1997.

1   D – The Shore Award has been presented annually since 1958 to honor the great Boston Bruins defenseman.

2   B – Gretzky recorded 163 assists in the 80-game schedule of the 1985-86 season.

3   D – Martin Havlat and Daniel Alfredsson both scored four times in a game against the Buffalo Sabres on November 2nd, 2005.

4   C – Known as the 'Makarov Rule' a player must be 26 or under to win the Calder Trophy.

5   D – Orr won the award in 1970.

6   C – Bernie Parent twice, Reggie Leach and Ron Hextall once, won the Conn Smythe Trophy as members of the Flyers.

7   A – Kurri scored 52 goals for the Edmonton Oilers in 1983-84.

8   C – Murdoch scored five times for the New York Rangers in a game against the Minnesota North Stars on October 12th, 1976.

9   D – Lemieux earned $11,350,000.00 for the Pittsburgh Penguins in 1996-97.

10 C – Morenz won the Hart Trophy in both 1931 and 1932.

11 A – Drury won the Hobey Baker Award in 1998 and the Calder Trophy in 1999.

12 D – Abel was given the rather unflattering nickname in the 1940s.

1   B – Wakely earned 16 shutouts in 334 games in the WHA.

2   A – The Islanders won the Stanley Cup in 1980, 1981, 1982 and 1983.

3   C – Lowe played 1037 games for the Oilers during his 13-year tenure with the club.

4   D – Bossy scored all four of the Islanders' game-winners in the 1983 Conference Final against the Boston Bruins.

5   B – Ashbee suffered a career-ending eye injury in 1974, prompting the Flyers to retire his jersey number 4.

6   D – Bower was named MVP of the American Hockey League in 1956, 1957 and 1958.

7   C – The Red Wings reached the 100-point plateau with 101 points during the 1950-51 season.

8   B – Bladon of the Philadelphia Flyers recorded eight points in a game against the Cleveland Barons on December 11th, 1977.

9   A – Forsberg led all scorers with 27 points despite his Colorado Avalanche's defeat in the Conference Final of the 2002 Stanley Cup Playoffs.

10 A – Gretzky won the Hart Trophy as a member of the Kings in 1989.

11 D – Sundin has been captain of the Toronto Maple Leafs since 1997.

12 B – Niedermayer played for the Blazers from 1989 until 1992.

1   D – The Canadiens lead all NHL teams in number of players inducted into the Hall of Fame.

2   D – Brent played for the Lightning in 1993-94 and 1994-95.

3   A – Barrasso was just 18 years old when he won the 1984 Calder Trophy as a member of the Buffalo Sabres.

4   B – Maki was not a member of the 'Scooter Line'.

5   C – Clark played for six NHL teams during his 15-year career.

6   A – The NHL introduced the rule to encourage teams to play for the regulation time win.

7   C – Henderson was not nearly as effective in the 1974 'Summit Series'.

8   B – Gretzky scored 12 short-handed goals in 1983-84 and 11 in 1984-85.

9   C – Heatley scored at least 50 goals for the Senators in both 2005-06 and 2006-07.

10   C – Mullen scored 502 goals in his 18 seasons in the NHL.

11   D – Ward won the Conn Smythe in 2006 as a member of the Carolina Hurricanes.

12   A – The fog in Buffalo's Memorial Auditorium was so bad that it frequently interrupted the Stanley Cup Final game.

1 D – Sather was behind the Oiler bench for their Stanley Cup victories in 1984, 1985, 1987 and 1988.

2 C – Thornton recorded at least 90 assists in both 2005-06 and 2006-07.

3 B – Gretzky led the NHL five times in goal scoring as a member of the Edmonton Oilers during the 1980s.

4 A – Hewitt was arguably the greatest broadcaster in hockey history.

5 C – Orr won the Hart, Art Ross, Norris and Conn Smythe trophies in 1970 as a member of the Boston Bruins.

6 A – Shanahan joined the Blues in the one-for-one deal.

7 B – Gordie Howe with six and Ted Lindsay with one are the only Red Wings to win the Art Ross Trophy.

8 A – Finland's Nittymaki was also named the top goaltender of the 2006 Winter Olympics.

9 B – Incredibly, Cournoyer played in ten Stanley Cup Final Series' with the Montreal Canadiens, all of which he won.

10 C – Rollins won the Hart Trophy in 1954 despite the fact that his Chicago Blackhawks finished last in the NHL in 1953-54.

11 A – Leetch scored 23 goals for the New York Rangers in 1988-89.

12 B – Esposito won 418 of his 423 career NHL victories as a member of the Chicago Blackhawks.

1   B – Armstrong played a total of 1187 regular season games for the Maple Leafs.

2   C – Lapointe scored 28 goals for the Habs during the 1974-75 season.

3   C – Sittler's historic game proved to be Reese's last game in the NHL.

4   D – Sillinger has played for 12 different teams as of the end of the 2007-08 season.

5   C – Sweden won the Olympic Gold in both 1994 and 2006.

6   A – Lindsay also went by the nickname 'Terrible Ted'.

7   B – Howe finished in the top five in NHL scoring from 1949-50 until 1969-70.

8   C – Richard scored five goals once and four goals twice during his Stanley Cup Playoff career.

9   B – Perreault is recognized as one of the greatest stick handlers in NHL history.

10 C – Pilous was behind the bench when the Blackhawks won their last Stanley Cup in 1961.

11 D – Messier won the Pearson Award in 1990 with the Edmonton Oilers and won it again in 1992 with the New York Rangers.

12 C – Thomas was a relatively short and stocky player who scored an impressive 411 goals during his NHL career.

1   D – Vachon ended his NHL career as a member of the Boston Bruins in 1981-82.

2   C – Fedorov won the Hart Trophy in 1994.

3   A – The Nordiques became the Colorado Avalanche to begin the 1995-96 season.

4   C – The Islanders retired Potvin's number 5 on February 1st, 1992.

5   A – Skrudlund of the Montreal Canadiens scored the fastest overtime goal in a playoff game against the Calgary Flames on May 18th, 1986.

6   B – The Conacher's were named in the First All-Star Team in 1933-34.

7   A – Richter of the New York Rangers won MVP honors in the 1994 NHL All-Star Game.

8   D – Both Calder Trophy winners played at Cornell.

9   D – Harvey's Montreal Canadien teammate Johnson won the 1959 Norris Trophy.

10   C – The Senators defeated the Boston Bruins to win the 1927 Stanley Cup.

11   C – Orr won MVP honors despite playing hurt the entire tournament.

12   B – 'The Russian Five' played an integral part in the Red Wings' Stanley Cup victories in 1997 and 1998.

QUIZ 56 Answers

1   B – Messier captained both the Edmonton Oilers and the New York Rangers to Stanley Cup Championships.

2   A – Ron was selected fourth overall by the Philadelphia Flyers and Rich was taken tenth overall by the Pittsburgh Penguins in the 1982 Entry Draft.

3   B – Bossy passed Richard as the Stanley Cup Playoff leading goal scorer in 1986.

4   A – Lemieux accomplished the feat in a game against the New Jersey Devils on December 31st, 1988.

5   B – Mikita played 22 seasons with the Blackhawks, recording a team record 1467 points during his career.

6   A – Howe won the Hart Trophy six times during the 1950s and 1960s as a member of the Detroit Red Wings.

7   D – Richards won the Conn Smythe Trophy in 2004.

8   A – Larmer played every game for the Blackhawks from October 6th, 1982 until April 15th, 1993.

9   B – Juneau recorded 70 assists for the Boston Bruins in 1992-93.

10 A – Potvin recorded his 1000th point of his NHL career on April 4th, 1987.

11 B – Leach won the Conn Smythe Trophy in 1976 despite the fact that his Philadelphia Flyers lost the Stanley Cup Final to the Montreal Canadiens.

12 C – Morenz was also nicknamed 'The Mitchell Meteor' and 'The Hurtling Hab' during his NHL career.

1   D – Nicholls recorded eight points for the Kings in a game against the Toronto Maple Leafs on December 1st, 1988.

2   C – Broten recorded 105 points for the Minnesota North Stars in 1985-86.

3   C – King coached the Canadian Olympic Team in 1984, 1988 and 1992.

4   B – Henri won the Stanley Cup 11 times while his older brother Maurice won it eight times.

5   D – Hossa recorded 100 points for the Thrashers in 2006-07.

6   B – Lemieux led the NHL in goal scoring in 1987-88, 1988-89 and 1995-96.

7   B – Smith was credited with a goal in a game against the Colorado Rockies on November 28th, 1979 when Rockies defenseman Rob Ramage shot the puck into his own net.

8   D – Coffey played for only three of the five Oiler Stanley Cup winning teams.

9   C – The Canadiens made it to the Stanley Cup Final from 1951 until 1960 inclusive.

10 A – The Maple Leafs Gaye Stewart in 1944, Gus Bodnar in 1945 and Frank McCool in 1946 won the Calder Trophy.

11 C – Potvin scored at least 20 goals in just 15 seasons with the New York Islanders.

12 A – Hull of the St. Louis Blues led the NHL in goal scoring in 1989-90, 1990-91 and 1991-92.

1 C – Hill scored three overtime goals in the 1939 Stanley Cup Playoffs for the Boston Bruins.

2 A – Yzerman won the Pearson Award in 1989.

3 D – Turco of the Dallas Stars was also named to the team.

4 D – MacInnis won the Conn Smythe Trophy in 1989.

5 C – Gainey won the Selke Trophy from 1978 until 1981 inclusive, the first four times the Selke Trophy was awarded.

6 C – The Petes have been a member of the OHL since 1956.

7 B – Vaive scored 54 goals for the Maple Leafs in 1981-82.

8 B – Hextall won both the Vezina and Conn Smythe trophies in 1987.

9 A – The Senators and the Lightning joined the NHL in 1992.

10 B – All three players were of Ukrainian descent.

11 D – Jose Theodore joined 11 other members of the Canadiens as the winner of the Hart Trophy in 2002.

12 A – Orr recorded 102 assists for the Boston Bruins during the 1970-71 season.

1 C – Makarov was 31 years old when he won the 1990 Calder Trophy as a member of the Calgary Flames.

2 B – Cole of the Carolina Hurricanes was awarded two penalty shots in a single game during the 2005-06 season.

3 A – Housley was just 20 years old when he scored 31 goals for the Buffalo Sabres in 1983-84.

4 A – The Oilers accomplished the feat 5 years in a row from 1981-82 until 1985-86.

5 C – Selanne of the Anaheim Mighty Ducks won NHL All-Star Game MVP honors in 1998.

6 B – Crosby won the Art Ross Trophy in 2006-07 at the age of 19.

7 A – Gainey won both trophies as a member of the Montreal Canadiens in 1979.

8 A – Hull scored 72 times in 1989-90, 86 in 1990-91 and 70 in 1991-92 as a member of the St. Louis Blues.

9 B – The Petes defeated the Brandon Wheat Kings in 1979 for their only Memorial Cup Championship.

10 D – Redmond scored 52 goals for the Red Wings in 1973-74.

11 B – Sakic led Canada to Olympic Gold in 2002.

12 D – Cheevers went undefeated in 32 straight games for the Boston Bruins in 1971-72.

QUIZ 60 Answers

1   D – Hasek was named to the NHL First All-Star Team in 1996-97, 1997-98 and 1998-99 as a member of the Buffalo Sabres.

2   A – The St. Patricks represented Toronto in the NHL from 1919-20 until 1926-27.

3   B – Ulf Nilsson recorded 484 points in 300 games for the Winnipeg Jets.

4   B – Phil Esposito, John Bucyk, Ken Hodge, Rick Middleton and Cam Neely all scored 50 goals in a season at least once for the Bruins.

5   C – The Penguins won 17 straight games from March 9th until April 10th, 1993.

6   A – Murphy played 1615 games in his 21 NHL seasons. Chelios should reach 1600 in 2008-09.

7   C – Kilrea has won well over 1000 games as the coach of the Ottawa 67s.

8   A – Heatley of the Atlanta Thrashers scored four times in the 2003 NHL All-Star Game.

9   C – Howe won the Patrick Award in 1967.

10 D – The Maple Leafs lost in the Stanley Cup Final in 1938, 1939 and 1940.

11 A – The Blues lost in the Stanley Cup Final in 1968, 1969 and 1970.

12 D – Richard scored 544 goals and added 421 assists for 965 points during his career with the Montreal Canadiens.

1 A – Lafleur was inducted into the Hall of Fame in 1988 and ended his NHL career in 1991.

2 D – Crosby was just 19 years old when he was named to the NHL First All-Star Team in 2006-07.

3 B – The 1948-49 Maple Leafs won 22 games and lost 25 yet managed to capture the 1949 Stanley Cup.

4 B – Goaltender Ranford was outstanding for Canada in being named Tournament MVP.

5 B – Lindsay led the NHL in goals in 1947-48, assists in 1949-50 and 1956-57, points in 1949-50 and penalty minutes in 1958-59.

6 C – Robitaille won the Calder Trophy in 1987.

7 D – Gretzky scored five goals in a game four times as a member of the Oilers.

8 B – Clapper played his all 20 of his NHL seasons with the Boston Bruins.

9 C – Esposito recorded 1590 points during his 18 seasons in the NHL.

10 A – Clancy was named to the NHL First All-Star Team in 1931 and 1934 as a member of the Toronto Maple Leafs.

11 B – Peca won the Selke Trophy in 1997 with the Buffalo Sabres and 2002 as a member of the New York Islanders.

12 D – Bouchard went by the nickname 'Butch'.

1 C – Sawchuk won 44 games for the Detroit Red Wings in 1950-51.

2 C – The Phoenix Coyotes selected Turris with the third pick overall in the 2007 Entry Draft.

3 D – Orr won both trophies in 1970 and 1972.

4 C – The leading scorer in the QMJHL has been awarded the Beliveau Trophy since 1969-70.

5 C – Stoughton scored 52 goals for the WHA's Cincinnati Stingers in 1976-77 and twice topped 50 with the NHLs Hartford Whalers, scoring 56 times in 1979-80 and 52 times in 1981-82.

6 D – The Toronto Maple Leafs' Horton was named to the 1963-64 First All-Star Team as a defenseman.

7 A – Stanley was relatively slow of foot, yet was considered a solid rearguard throughout his 21-year NHL career.

8 A – Bossy scored 53 times for the New York Islanders in 1977-78.

9 D – The Senators chose Spezza with the second pick of the 2001 Entry Draft.

10 D – Harvey was selected to the NHL First All-Star Team nine times as a Montreal Canadien and once as a New York Ranger.

11 A – Oates recorded 1420 points during his NHL career.

12 B – Gretzky won the Lady Byng Trophy five times in his glorious career.

1   C – Neely scored 50 goals in just 49 games for the Boston Bruins in 1993-94.

2   A – Orr won NHL All-Star MVP honors in 1972.

3   B – Pierre Pilote won the Norris Trophy three times as a Blackhawk while Chris Chelios won it twice and Doug Wilson won it once.

4   A – Brown of the Kamloops Blazers recorded 212 points during the 1986-87 season.

5   B – Bossy recorded 35 points for the New York Islanders during the 1981 Stanley Cup Playoff.

6   A – The Detroit franchise was known as the Falcons from 1930 until 1932.

7   B – Gadsby recorded his 500th NHL point in 1962-63 as a member of the Detroit Red Wings.

8   B – Bondra scored the four goals in just 4:12 in a game against the Tampa Bay Lightning on February 5th, 1994.

9   C – Francis played 1731 regular season games during his 23-year NHL career.

10   D – Bure won the Calder Trophy in 1992.

11   C – Richards scored seven game-winning goals for the Tampa Bay Lightning during the 2004 Stanley Cup Playoffs.

12   D – Iginla would win the Art Ross Trophy in 2002 with 96 points.

1. A – Stevens finished runner-up in Norris Trophy voting in both 1988 and 1994.

2. C – Richard led the NHL in goal scoring in 1944-45, 1946-47, 1949-50, 1953-54 and 1954-55.

3. C – Lemieux won back to back Conn Smythe trophies in 1991 and 1992.

4. D – Dennis Hull had perhaps a harder shot than his brother Bobby but his accuracy left a lot to be desired.

5. B – Belfour was named to the NHL First All-Star Team in 1990-91 as a member of the Chicago Blackhawks.

6. C – Giguere won the Conn Smythe Trophy in 2003 and his Anaheim Ducks would win the 2007 Stanley Cup.

7. B – Worsley also won 335 games during his 21-year NHL career.

8. D – Shack scored at least 20 times in a season for Toronto, Boston, Los Angeles, Buffalo and Pittsburgh.

9. D – The Blues selected Gilmour with the 134th pick of the 1982 Entry Draft.

10. A – Morrow won a Gold Medal with the United States and a Stanley Cup with the New York Islanders in 1980.

11. A – Robinson won the Norris Trophy in both 1977 and 1980.

12. B – Mikita won all three trophies in both 1967 and 1968.

1   A – Lumley was just 17 years old when he played his first NHL game.

2   C – Mario Lemieux with six, Jaromir Jagr with four and Sidney Crosby with one have combined to win 11 Art Ross trophies.

3   C – Lemieux recorded at least one point in 46 consecutive games during the 1989-90 season.

4   B – Professionals were first allowed in the Olympic Games in 1988 with the Soviet Union capturing the Gold Medal.

5   D – Jagr's first name Jaromir is an anagram for 'Mario Jr.'.

6   B – Park was runner-up in Norris Trophy voting to Bobby Orr in 1970, 1971 and 1972.

7   C – Williams spent 3966 minutes in the penalty box in his 14-year NHL career.

8   C – Esposito won the Art Ross Trophy from 1970-71 until 1973-74 inclusive.

9   A – Bower was named to the NHL First All-Star Team in 1960-61.

10   B – Lindbergh won the Vezina Trophy in 1985 as a member of the Philadelphia Flyers.

11   D – Nighbor was born in Pembroke, Ontario on January 26th, 1893.

12   B – Burns coached the Montreal Canadiens, Toronto Maple Leafs, Boston Bruins and the New Jersey Devils during his NHL coaching career.

1   B – Mark Howe recorded 92 career points during the WHA Playoffs.

2   B – Orr led the NHL in assists five times during the 1970s.

3   C – McDonald's number 9 was the first jersey retired by the Flames.

4   B – Pronger of the Edmonton Oilers scored on Cam Ward of the Carolina Hurricanes in the 2006 Stanley Cup Final.

5   A – Kurri scored 19 times for the Edmonton Oilers during the 1985 Stanley Cup Playoffs.

6   C – Shack was always entertaining especially to the fans of the Toronto Maple Leafs.

7   D – Sanderson's pass from behind the net allowed Orr to beat St. Louis Blues goaltender Glenn Hall with the Stanley Cup winning goal.

8   C – Gretzky played his first eight games as a professional with the Racers in 1978-79.

9   B – Esposito of the Chicago Blackhawks shared the Vezina with Parent.

10   C – Andreychuk scored 29 goals for the Buffalo Sabres and 25 goals for the Toronto Maple Leafs during the 1992-93 season.

11   D – Bodnar of the Toronto Maple Leafs scored the record-setting goal in a game against the New York Rangers on October 30th, 1943.

12   C – Berard was selected first overall by the Ottawa Senators in 1995 and won the Calder Trophy as a New York Islander in 1997.

1   B – Gretzky totaled 37 three-goal games, nine four-goal games and four five-goal games during his 20-year NHL career.

2   D – 2006 Stanley Cup Finalists, Edmonton Oilers and Carolina Hurricanes both failed to reach the 2007 Stanley Cup Playoffs.

3   A – Sakic earned $15,000,000 for the Colorado Avalanche in 1997-98.

4   D – Jean Pronovost, Pierre Larouche, Mike Bullard, Rick Kehoe, Mario Lemieux, Jaromir Jagr and Kevin Stevens all scored at least 50 goals in a season at least once for the Penguins.

5   B – Berenson scored six goals for the St. Louis Blues in a game against the Philadelphia Flyers on November 7th, 1968.

6   D – Simmer of the Los Angeles Kings scored 17 goals during his incredible streak.

7   B – Kelly won the Lady Byng Trophy three times as a defenseman with the Detroit Red Wings and once as a forward with the Toronto Maple Leafs.

8   B – The Sabres scored nine 2nd-period goals in a game against the Toronto Maple Leafs on March 19th, 1981.

9   B – Richard played for the Habs, 1955 until 1975.

10   D – Hull scored his 50th goal in his 49th game in 1990-91 and his 50th goal of the 1991-92 season in his 50th game.

11   A – Bellows, at age 19, replaced the injured Craig Hartsburg for the remainder of the 1983-84 season as captain of the Minnesota North Stars.

12   B – Bower backstopped the Toronto Maple Leafs to four Stanley Cup Championships during the 1960s.